Scientific Theories, Laws, and Principles

Authors: Schrylet Cameron and Carolyn Craig

Editors: Mary Dieterich and Sarah M. Anderson

Proofreader: Margaret Brown

COPYRIGHT © 2011 Mark Twain Media, Inc.

ISBN 978-1-58037-581-8

Printing No. CD-404151

Mark Twain Media, Inc., Publishers
Distributed by Carson-Dellosa Publishing LLC

Visit us at www.carsondellosa.com

Table of Contents

Introduction to the Teacher

Scientific Theories, Laws, and Principles is written for classroom teachers, parents, and students. The book describes the concepts that define the basic science studied by middle-school students. Textbooks often present more information than students can process. This book presents the concepts in an easy-to-read and easy-to-understand format that does not overwhelm the learner. The text presents only the most important information in small bites to make it easier for students to comprehend. Vocabulary words are boldfaced. Hands-on activities help clarify concepts introduced in the unit and can be completed individually or in a group setting. Labs focus on applying science concepts using the steps in the scientific method.

This book was specifically designed to facilitate planning for the diverse learning styles and skill levels of middle-school students. Each lesson can be used as an individual lesson or to supplement existing textbooks or curriculum programs. This book can be used as an enhancement to what is being done in the classroom or as a tutorial at home. Each unit provides the teacher with alternative methods of instruction.

- **Reading Exercises** introduce the basic lesson concepts.
- **Knowledge Builder** pages develop and expand concepts introduced in the reading exercise.
- **Understanding Formulas** pages present the formula connected with the concept and provide practice in using the formula to solve real-world problems.
- **Apply** pages assess student understanding of lesson concepts using selected response (multiple choice and fill in the blanks), constructed response (closed-ended), and critical thinking (open-ended) questioning strategies.
- **Investigate** pages use simple hands-on activities to strengthen understanding of lesson concepts.
- **Inquiry Labs** provide opportunities for students to expand learning by practicing the steps in the scientific method.

Scientific Theories, Laws, and Principles is an overview of scientific principles, laws, and theories that make an impact on every facet of our daily lives. Student knowledge and understanding of these concepts strengthen scientific literacy skills. The units are correlated to the National Science Education Standards (NSES) and the National Council for Teachers of Mathematics Standards (NCTM).

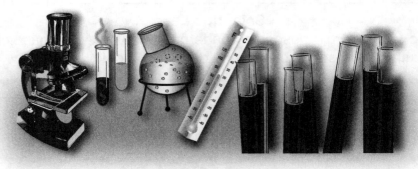

Science Overview

What Is Science?
Science is a way to learn about the natural world through observations.

What Do Scientists Do?
Scientists ask many questions. They observe, infer, and predict to learn more about the natural world.

Scientific Method
Scientists use a process to find answers to questions they have about the world around them. This process is called the **scientific method** or scientific inquiry. They use the steps in the scientific method to design and conduct scientific investigations to explore possible answers.

Steps in the scientific method answer a question.

1. <u>Purpose</u>: What do you want to learn from the experiment?
2. <u>Research</u>: What is already known about the topic?
3. <u>Hypothesis</u>: What do you think will happen in the experiment?
4. <u>Procedure</u>: How will you test the hypothesis and record the results?
5. <u>Analysis</u>: What do the results tell you?
6. <u>Conclusion</u>: Do the results support your hypothesis?

Scientific Theory
Scientists might consider scientific theories before answering questions. A **scientific theory** ties many observations together. They are not someone's guesses or opinions; they are based on ideas that have been tested and shown to be true over time. A theory can be changed if enough new data doesn't support it.

Scientific Law
A **scientific law** is a rule describing patterns in nature. A law has scientific proof and stands to be the truth until observations are made that do not follow the law.

Scientific Principle
A **scientific principle** is the same as a scientific law.

UNIT 1: SCIENTIFIC THEORIES
Lesson 1: Atomic Theory of Matter

Atomic Theory

The **Atomic Theory** is the idea that matter is made up of tiny units called atoms.

Democritus and Dalton

Greek philosopher Democritus came up with the idea that atoms existed. He believed matter could only be broken down so far and then no further. These small particles were called *atoma*, or "indivisible particles." He believed atoms were like mini solar systems, with tiny planets orbiting a tiny sun. However, his ideas were not accepted for over 2,000 years.

Then, in the early 1800s, John Dalton developed the Atomic Theory. All current understanding about atoms is based on his model. Dalton's model was a set of ideas.

- Matter was made of atoms that were too small to be seen by the human eye.

- Each type of matter was made of only one kind of atom.

Dalton's Model of the Atom

Matter is made of atoms. You just can't see them!

Democritus (460 B.C.–370 B.C.) was the first person to develop Atomic Theory.

Atoms are too small to see.

John Dalton (1766–1844) used symbols to represent elements.

◯	Oxygen	Ⓢ	Silver
⊙	Hydrogen	⊛	Mercury
⊘	Nitrogen	Ⓒ	Copper
⚫	Carbon	Ⓘ	Iron
⊕	Sulfur	Ⓝ	Nickel
☮	Phosphorus	Ⓣ	Tin
Ⓖ	Gold	Ⓛ	Lead
Ⓟ	Platinum	Ⓩ	Zinc

ATOMIC THEORY OF MATTER
Knowledge Builder

Models of the Atom

Thomson

In the 1890s, J. J. Thomson discovered the **electron**. Many of his experiments with the cathode ray led him to believe in the existence of an atomic particle "with a mass about 1,000 times smaller than a hydrogen atom." As Thomson lectured to scholars in England and America, his ideas met with much skepticism. The lack of support from his colleagues caused him to work even harder to prove what he knew existed—the electron.

Thomson's "Plum Pudding" Model

Negative electron "plums" in a positive "pudding"

Rutherford

In 1919, Ernest Rutherford discovered the **proton**, and as he continued testing ideas, he developed the idea of the nucleus of the atom. He also proposed the idea of another particle (the neutron), which would be located in the nucleus with the proton. He was certain that both positive and negative charges were emitted by the atom. Since Thomson had identified the existence of the negatively charged electron, Rutherford proposed the idea of a positively charged proton. With further studies, he found that each of these particles were found in a specific location relative to one another, and he drew models to represent his ideas.

Rutherford's Nuclear Atom Model

Protons and neutrons in a nucleus with electrons orbiting outside the nucleus

Chadwick

James Chadwick, a student of Rutherford's, is credited with the discovery of the **neutron**. Chadwick used the work of others to successfully determine that the neutron did exist and that its mass was about 0.1 percent more than the proton's.

Chadwick Discovers Neutrons

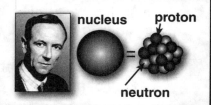

Bohr

The first atom model to gain acceptance was one proposed by Niels Bohr in the 1920s, which suggested electrons move in **energy levels**. Bohr was a student of J.J. Thomson and won the Nobel Prize in physics in 1922 for his model. He was only 37 years old at the time of the award.

Bohr's Atomic Model

Positively charged nucleus with electrons in specific energy levels

ATOMIC THEORY OF MATTER
Knowledge Builder

Matter, Atoms, and Elements

Matter

Matter is the term we use to explain anything that has mass and takes up space. All objects and substances are made of matter. Matter isn't always visible to the naked eye. Air is also matter. There are three **states of matter**: solids, liquids, and gases. A fourth state called plasma exists, but it is found only on the sun.

 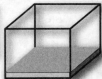 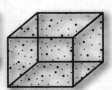

Solid	Liquid	Gas
Holds shape	Takes shape	Takes shape
Fixed volume	of container	and volume
	Fixed volume	of container

Atom

An **atom** is the simplest form of matter that cannot be changed into a simpler form by ordinary means. Everything in our world is made of atoms, and this explains why atoms are called the building blocks of matter. An atom is made up of electrons, protons, and neutrons. The **nucleus** (positively charged, center part of the atom) is made of two kinds of particles: protons and neutrons. **Protons** have a positive charge, and **neutrons** are neutral, having no charge. **Electrons** have a negative charge, and they circle the nucleus of the atom.

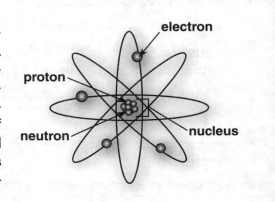

Element

An **element** is a substance made entirely of the same type of atoms. There are at least 118 known elements, and about 90 of them occur naturally on Earth. These elements include gases in the air, minerals in rocks, and liquids such as mercury. The other elements are called synthetic elements; this means that they are made in a laboratory. Elements are listed in a periodic table.

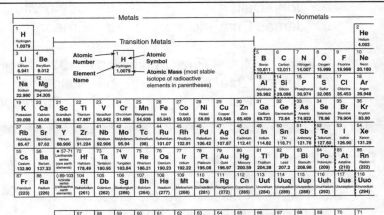

Name: _____ Date: _____

ATOMIC THEORY OF MATTER
Apply

Matching

_____ 1. nucleus

_____ 2. energy levels

_____ 3. matter

_____ 4. element

_____ 5. atom

_____ 6. protons

a. the simplest form of matter

b. have a positive charge

c. the locations where electrons orbit

d. positively charged, center part of an atom

e. a substance made up of entirely the same type of atoms

f. anything that has mass and takes up space

Fill in the Blanks

1. Greek philosopher _____ came up with the idea that atoms existed.

2. _____ have a negative charge, and they circle the nucleus of the atom.

3. The four states of matter are _____, _____, _____, and _____.

4. The _____ _____ is the idea that matter is made up of tiny units called atoms.

5. _____ have a positive charge, and _____ are neutral, having no charge.

Multiple Choice

1. This scientist discovered the proton.
   a. John Dalton
   c. James Chadwick
   b. Democritus
   d. Ernest Rutherford

2. He won the Nobel Prize in physics in 1922 for his atomic model.
   a. James Chadwick
   c. Ernest Rutherford
   b. Niels Bohr
   d. J.J. Thomson

Constructed Response
Answer on your own paper.
1. J.J. Thomson discovered the electron. What did Niels Bohr suggest about electrons?
2. What contribution did John Dalton make to science?

Critical Thinking
Answer on your own paper.

Why is the word *atom* an appropriate term for Democritus' idea?

Name: _____ Date: _____

ATOMIC THEORY OF MATTER
Investigate

Activity #1–Physical Properties of Matter
Directions: Fill the data table below by observing five objects in your classroom. Physical properties of matter are characteristics that can be observed, such as color, shape, smell, taste, and texture.

Object	Color	Texture	Shape	Smell	Taste
1.					
2.					
3.					
4.					
5.					

Activity #2–3-D Model of an Atom
Directions: Create a three-dimensional model of an atom that can be hung from a string. Select an element from the list below. Use the periodic table to determine your element's atomic number. Using the information, make a detailed sketch of the atom. Make sure to display the correct number of neutrons, electrons, and protons; these should be in their correct locations. Next, decide what to use to represent the neutrons, elections, and protons. Anything small, round, and that can be glued to each other will work, such as ping-pong balls, small rubber balls, or styrofoam balls. Color-code the balls so that it is easier to identify the protons, neutrons, and electrons. The electrons should be smaller than the protons and neutrons.

Elements
hydrogen
sodium
copper
carbon
calcium
gold

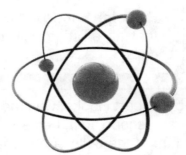

Activity #3–Element Symbols
Directions: Look at John Dalton's symbols for elements on page 3. Choose five elements and use your own symbols to represent them.

Element	My Symbol
1.	
2.	
3.	
4.	
5.	

UNIT 1: SCIENTIFIC THEORIES
Lesson 2: Cell Theory

Credit for developing the Cell Theory is usually given to the three of us.

Theodor Schwann   **Matthias Schleiden**   **Rudolf Virchow**

Cell Theory

The **Cell Theory** is a widely accepted explanation of the relationship between cells and living things. The cell theory states:

- All living things or organisms are made of cells.
- New cells are created by old cells dividing into two cells.
- Cells are the basic building units of life.

Building Blocks of Life

Cells, the "building blocks of life," are the smallest living things. All organisms are made up of cells. Some living things are unicellular and carry out all the basic life activities within that single cell. However, most living things are multicellular.

Cell Discoveries

- **Robert Hooke** (1665–1703) was the first person to see cells with the aid of an early compound microscope. Hooke looked at a slice of cork and saw small, empty, box-like structures. He thought the box shapes resembled cells, or rooms, monks used for sleeping. He decided to name the structures cells.

- **Anton Van Leeuwenhoek** (1632–1723) was the first person to observe living cells. He studied pond water and observed single-celled organisms.

- **Matthias Schledien** (1804–1881) was a botanist who discovered living plants were made up of cells with a nuclei.

- **Theodor Schwann** (1810–1882) was a zoologist who discovered that animals are made up of cells with nuclei.

- **Rudolph Vichow** (1821–1902) believed that an existing cell divided to form new cells.

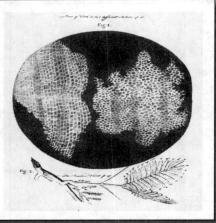

At right is the drawing of the structure of cork by Robert Hooke that appeared in *Micrographia.*

Published in 1665, *Micrographia,* a book by Robert Hooke, was the first scientific bestseller. It detailed Hooke's observations using his microscope. In it, he used the term "cells." He explained that the boxlike cells of cork reminded him of the cells of a monastery. He reported observing similar structures in wood and in other plants.

CELL THEORY
Knowledge Builder

Cells

Organisms

All organisms are made up of cells.

- **Multicelluar** organisms are made up of many cells.
- **Unicellular** organisms have one cell.

Example: Snails, fish, and humans are multicellular. Many organisms, including bacteria, are unicellular.

Exceptions

Viruses are an exception to the Cell Theory. They are considered alive by some scientists, yet they are not made up of cells. Viruses have many features of life, but by definition of the Cell Theory, they are not alive. They are basically made up of proteins.

Types of Cells

There are two main types of cells.

- A **eukaryotic cell** is a single cell with a nucleus.
- A **prokaryotic cell** is the simplest type of cell. The cell has no nucleus. DNA and other materials float "freely" inside the cytoplasm.

Example: All organisms except bacteria are made up of eukaryotic cells. Bacteria are prokaryotic cells.

Three Main Parts of a Cell

All eukaryotic cells have three things in common. They all have a **cell membrane**, **nucleus**, and **cytoplasm**.

Nucleus
- controls all the cell activities
- round or egg-shaped structure
- found near the center of the cell
- dark in color
- contains DNA

Cell Membrane
- thin layer that encloses the cell
- controls movement of material into and out of the cell
- provides shape and protection for the cell

Cytoplasm
- gel-like material
- contains proteins, nutrients, and all the other cell organelles

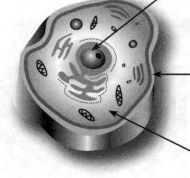

Animal Cell

Plant Cell

Name: _____   Date: _____

CELL THEORY
Apply

Matching

_____ 1. cell   a. exception to the Cell Theory

_____ 2. multicellular   b. controls cell activity

_____ 3. prokaryotic cell   c. organisms made up of many cells

_____ 4. nucleus   d. smallest living thing

_____ 5. virus   e. has no nucleus; DNA and other materials float freely
                                       inside the cytoplasm

Fill in the Blanks

1. All eukaryotic cells have three things in common. They all have a _____
   _____, _____, and _____.

2. All living things or organisms are made of _____.

3. _____ _____ was the first person to see cells with the aid of
   an early compound microscope.

4. Cells are the basic building _____ of life.

5. Anton Van Leeuwenhoek was the first person to observe _____ cells.

Constructed Response

1. If you were looking at a cell under the microscope, how would you know if it was a eukaryotic
   cell? _____
   _____

2. Why do scientists classify bacteria as unicellular? _____
   _____

Critical Thinking

Why do you think some scientists do not consider viruses cells?

_____

_____

_____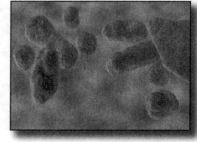

_____

_____

Name: _____   Date: _____

CELL THEORY
Investigate

Activity—Gelatin Cell Model

Materials:
> 2 plastic resealable sandwich bags
> raisins
> 2 half-pint milk cartons (with tops removed)
> celery, cubed
> 2 packages lemon gelatin
> 2 cups boiling water
> 2 cups cold water

Procedure:
Day 1
Step #1: Line the milk cartons with the sandwich bags, allowing the excess part of the bag to extend over the edges of the milk carton.
Step #2: Stir 1 box of gelatin into 1 cup boiling water until dissolved. Stir in 1 cup cold water.
Step #3: When the gelatin has cooled but not gelled, pour 1/2 cup into each lined carton.
Step #4: When the mixture begins to gel, gently push a raisin (nucleus) into the gelatin of each bag. Gently push several celery cubes (chloroplasts) into one bag of gelatin. Refrigerate each box of gelatin overnight.

celery cubes

Day2
Step #1: Prepare a second batch of gelatin mixture. Slowly add 1/2 cup of the cooled mixture to each milk carton.
Step #2: Once the mixture has completely cooled, close the sandwich bag.
Step #3: Refrigerate the cartons of gelatin until the gelatin is firm.
Step #4: Leave the sandwich bag with the celery cubes in the carton. Take the other sandwich bag out of the carton.

Conclusion:
Which model represents an animal cell and which represents a plant cell? Explain your answer.

_____

_____

_____

UNIT 2: SCIENTIFIC LAWS
Lesson 1: Periodic Law

Periodic Law

The **Periodic Law** states that an element's properties depend upon its atomic weight.

Dmitri Mendelèev

In 1869, a Russian scientist by the name of Dmitri Mendelèev constructed the first Periodic Table. Mendelèev's table contained the 63 elements known during his time. He left gaps in the Periodic Table to show that there were still more elements to be discovered. His Periodic Table looked very much like the one that we use today.

I predict that elements will be discovered to fill those missing holes in my table!

Dmitri Mendelèev (1834–1907) was a Russian chemist credited with creating the Periodic Table in 1869.

The Periodic Table

The **Periodic Table** was first constructed in 1869 to organize the 63 known elements by their properties. The current standard table contains 118 elements. They are organized by their families, atomic numbers, and many other properties.

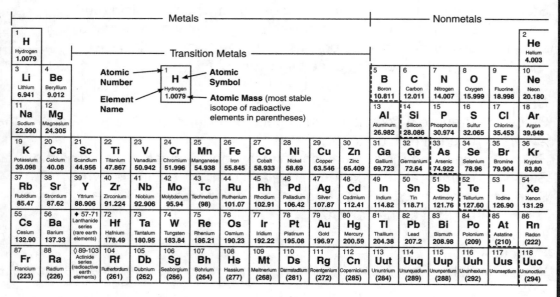

PERIODIC LAW
Knowledge Builder

The Periodic Table organizes elements by their properties.

Families

Each vertical column on the Periodic Table is an element **family**. All of the elements in each family have similar properties. They usually react the same in chemical reactions, and they may even look the same and be used for the same purposes. Each family is numbered and has a name.

Periods

Each horizontal row is called a **period**. There are seven periods on the Periodic Table. The lanthanides and actinides really fit in with the sixth and seventh periods. They have been written at the bottom of the table for convenience.

Metals, Nonmetals, and Metalloids

Some Periodic Tables show a bold line in the shape of steps on the right side of the Periodic Table. All the elements to the left of that line are metals. **Metals** are elements that are good conductors of heat and electricity. They have a shiny, metallic luster. Metals can also be pounded into shapes or drawn into wire. All of the elements to the right of the bold step-shaped line are called nonmetals. **Nonmetals** are poor conductors of heat and electricity. They usually have a dull or earthy luster. When pounded, nonmetals usually shatter or form powders. The elements that touch the bold step-shaped line are called **metalloids**. These elements have characteristics of both metals and nonmetals.

Solid, Liquid, or Gas

Some Periodic Tables even tell us whether an element is a solid, liquid, or gas at room temperature. Most elements are solids. There are a few gases. Only mercury and bromine are liquids at room temperature.

Radioactivity

Radioactive means that the element naturally gives off particles. All the elements with an atomic number of 84 or greater are radioactive. Technetium (43) and promethium (61) also have no stable form. All elements have radioactive forms, and most elements have stable forms. Some Periodic Tables show whether an element is radioactive or stable.

Natural or Manmade

Natural elements occur somewhere in nature. **Synthetic** elements are elements that are made by humans in laboratories. Many of the heavier elements are synthetic. All of the elements with an atomic number of 95 or greater are synthetic. Some Periodic Tables show whether an element is natural or synthetic.

PERIODIC LAW
Knowledge Builder

Boxes in the Periodic Table

Atomic Number

Every element has an **atomic number**. This is the number of protons in its atom. A proton is a positively charged particle in an atom. For example, the element copper has 29 protons in its atom. If you read the Periodic Table left to right and row by row, the atomic numbers will increase in order until you get to number 57. This is because elements 58–71 and 90–103 appear in order in the two rows at the bottom of the Periodic Table, which are called the lanthanides and actinides.

Symbol

Each element is assigned a **symbol**. The symbol usually corresponds to the element's name. Symbols are usually two letters. However, some symbols have one or three letters. The first letter of the symbol is capitalized, and the rest of the letters are lowercase.

$$Xe = Xenon$$
$$C = Carbon$$

Boxes

Each box on the Periodic Table has the atomic number, which represents the number of protons or positively charged particles in the nucleus. The number of electrons always equals the number of protons in an electrically balanced atom. Atoms of the same element have the same number of protons but may have a different number of neutrons. Elements with different numbers of neutrons are called **isotopes**. **Atomic weights** are determined by comparing the element with an atom of carbon 12, which is assigned the weight of 12 units. The atomic mass numbers are often used in place of atomic weights. **Atomic mass** is the number of protons and neutrons found in the atom.

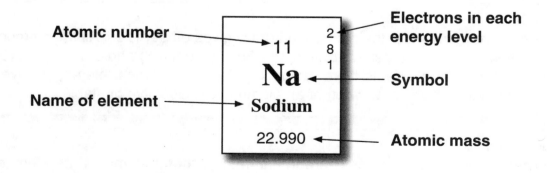

PERIODIC LAW
Knowledge Builder

Organization of the Periodic Table

Group 1: The Alkali Metal Family

The alkali metal family is found on the Periodic Table in Group 1, which is on the far left side of the table. The metals in this group are lithium, sodium, potassium, rubidium, cesium, and francium. The gas hydrogen is also put in this group because of its reactivity.

All of the metals in this group are soft, silvery-white metals with low melting points. These metals, along with hydrogen, are extremely reactive. Hydrogen will blow up upon any contact with flames. The metals are so reactive that they will burn the skin if touched. They tarnish rapidly. The metals in this family react violently with water. They easily form salts with the halogens. They are never found in their pure forms in nature. They are easy to identify because they each give off a different color when they burn. Lithium flames are a crimson color, sodium flames are yellow, potassium flames are violet, rubidium flames are reddish-violet, and cesium flames are blue. Little is known about francium because it is so rare and radioactive.

The alkali metal family has many important uses. Lithium is used in grease and other lubricants. It is also used in aircraft parts and batteries. Sodium is found in salt and used in gasoline. Potassium is more expensive than sodium and is less widely used. Potassium is used in fertilizer and photography.

Group 2: The Alkaline Earth Metal Family

The alkaline earth metal family is found on the Periodic Table in Group 2, which is on the far left side of the table between Group 1, the alkali metals, and Groups 3-12, the transition elements. This family is made up of six metals (beryllium, magnesium, calcium, strontium, barium, and radium).

The metals in this family are all soft and silvery-white in color. They have high melting points and high densities. They are reactive. They will react with water. They can be handled by humans. These metals will oxidize or tarnish in air. They are never found in nature in their pure forms. They are good conductors of electricity. Each element of this family burns in a different color. Magnesium will give off a bright white light. Calcium flames are an orange-red. Strontium flames give off a bright red color. Barium will burn with a yellowish-green color. Radium gives off a vivid crimson color when it burns.

The alkaline earth metals are used in fireworks because of their bright colors when they burn. Beryllium is often added to other metals to make hard metal alloys. Beryllium is also used to make rocket nose cones. Beryllium is used in nuclear reactors. Magnesium is used in aircraft and photographic equipment. Calcium is used with other metals to make reactive alloys. Radium is radioactive and is used in the treatment of cancer.

Groups 3–12: The Transition Element Family

The transition element family is found in the middle of the Periodic Table in Groups 3–12. The transition element family is by far the largest family on the Periodic Table with 40 members. Some of the more common and widely-used members of this family include iron, nickel, copper, zinc, silver, and gold.

The transition elements are all metals; that's why they are sometimes called the transition metals. Most of the elements in this family are hard, strong, and shiny metals. Most of them have very high melting points and boiling points. Mercury is one exception; it is a liquid at room temperature. Most transition elements are good conductors of heat and electricity. Most transition elements will dissolve in acid. Gold is one exception; it resists acids. Most transition elements can bond to oxygen in more ways than one, making different compounds. Iron is a good example of this behavior. Iron bonds with oxygen to form the ores hematite and magnetite. Both ores have different ratios of oxygen and iron. Most of these elements can be pounded into shapes and drawn into wires. Most of the transition elements can form colored compounds with oxygen. Zinc, titanium, and chromium form many colored compounds with oxygen.

The transition elements have many uses because of their ability to form strong metal alloys, their ability to be pounded into shapes, their ability to be drawn into wires, and their beauty. It is because of these abilities that transition elements are used in construction materials, pipes, wires, coins, jewelry, aircraft, cars, bicycles, cooking utensils, and many other items. Many transition elements are used to manufacture widely-used compounds, such as cleaners. Many transition elements are used in catalytic converters, which help control the pollution in car exhaust. Transition elements are also added to paints to give them color.

Groups 13–16: The BCNO Family

The BCNO family is found on the right side of the Periodic Table between the transition elements (Group 3–12) and the halogens (Group 17). The BCNO family is a very large family with 25 members. Some of the more common members of this family include carbon, nitrogen, oxygen, aluminum, silicon, sulfur, arsenic, tin, and lead.

The BCNO family is given its name because of the symbols of the lightest elements in each column of the family: boron (B), carbon (C), nitrogen (N), and oxygen (0). The members of this family are metals, nonmetals, or metalloids. Some members of this family are gases at room temperature (nitrogen and oxygen), but most are solids. They are reactive but are selective with which elements they will bond. Most will bond with oxygen. Oxygen will even bond with itself. There are no hard and fast rules that fit all the elements of this family except that the members of each column tend to bond with other elements in a similar fashion.

There are a wide variety of uses for the BCNO family. This is because there are a wide variety of elements. Many of the elements of the BCNO family are essential to life (carbon, oxygen, nitrogen, and phosphorus). The metals in this family are used in the electronics industry. Silicon and germanium are used in computers. The nonmetals in this family are used as insulators on wires because they will not conduct electricity. Some members in this family are used as poisons, fertilizers, in scuba gear, soap, glass-making, solder, aircraft, and weapons. Aluminum is a member of this family with many uses, including drink cans, foil, pots, and pans.

Group 17: The Halogen Family

The elements of Group 17, the halogens, are found on the right side of the Periodic Table between Groups 13–16 (the BCNO family) and Group 18 (the noble gases). The halogens are a very small family consisting of only five elements (fluorine, chlorine, bromine, iodine, and astatine).

The halogens are a family of poisonous nonmetals. At room temperature, fluorine and chlorine are gases, bromine is a liquid, and iodine and astatine are solids. The halogens are very reactive and are never found in their pure forms in nature. The reactivity of the halogens decreases as atomic number increases. The halogens are poor conductors of electricity. The halogens will combine with the alkali metals to form a family of chemical compounds called salts.

The halogen family has a variety of uses. Fluorine is added to toothpaste and water to prevent tooth decay. Fluorine will combine with uranium to form nuclear fuel. Chlorine is added to water supplies and swimming pools to kill germs. Chlorine is widely used in bleach and salt. Bromine is used as a gasoline additive, photograph developer, fire  retardant, and an insecticide. Bromine is also used to kill germs in water supplies. Iodine is added to salt to reduce thyroid disease. Iodine is also used as a film developer and as a disinfectant in water supplies. Astatine is very rare, very radioactive, and has no uses.

Group 18: The Noble Gases

The noble gases are found in the far right column of the Periodic Table just to the right of Group 17, the halogens. The noble gases are a family of six gases: helium, neon, argon, krypton, xenon, and radon.

All of the members of the noble gas family are colorless, tasteless, and odorless gases. They are extremely nonreactive. Helium, neon, and argon will not combine with other elements. Xenon, krypton, and radon will combine with other elements, but this is a very difficult process to perform. When an electrical current is passed through one of these gases, it will glow in a characteristic color. Neon has a characteristic orange-red glow.

Helium is lighter than air and is used in balloons and blimps. Neon, argon, krypton, and xenon are used in lights because of the colors they make and in light bulbs because they do not react with the metal (usually tungsten) that makes up the filament. Radon is radioactive and is used in the treatment of cancer.

The Lanthanide Series

The lanthanide series of elements is found at the bottom of the Periodic Table. This series appears in the top of the bottom two rows. It consists of 15 elements, including lanthanum.

Every member of the lanthanide series is a soft, silvery metal. These metals are reactive and will burn in oxygen or air. They will oxidize or tarnish rapidly in air. The lanthanide series metals are similar to the metals in the transition elements family, except they are poor conductors of electricity. The lanthanides all react in a similar manner, and it is because of this that they are found together in nature. Lanthanides produce a spark when struck.

Lanthanide alloys made with iron are used to make flints for cigarette lighters because of their ability to produce a spark. Several of the metals in this series are used in glass, welders' goggles, nuclear reactors, and the petroleum industry. Many of the lanthanides are used in color television screens and computer monitors because they produce colors when combined with phosphorus. Some examples of the colors produced by lanthanides include red from europium and green from terbium

The Actinide Series

The actinide series of elements is found in the very bottom row of the Periodic Table. This series is made of 15 elements, including actinium and uranium.

The members of the actinide series are all radioactive. All of the actinides are silvery metals. All of the elements in the actinide series are reactive. Actinium, thorium, protactinium, and uranium are all natural. Neptunium and plutonium were once thought to be only synthetic, but small amounts have been found in nature. All other members of this series are synthetic. All of the actinides after curium are very radioactive and have been produced in such small amounts that little is known about these elements.

Uranium is by far the most stable actinide. It is used as a fuel for nuclear power plants and nuclear weapons. Uranium is also used as a pigment in glass and ceramics. Plutonium is used in nuclear weapons and to power space-exploration equipment. Curium is used to power satellites and was used to test moon soils. Americium is used in smoke detectors.

Name: _____ Date: _____

PERIODIC LAW
Apply

Matching
_____ 1. Periodic Table
_____ 2. Periodic Law
_____ 3. atomic number
_____ 4. symbol
_____ 5. atomic mass

a. the number of protons in an atom of the element
b. two or three letters that correspond to the element's name
c. states that an element's properties depend upon its atomic weight
d. the number of protons and neutrons found in the atom
e. organizes the 118 known elements by their families, atomic numbers, and many other properties

Fill in the Blanks
1. The _____ elements are all metals.
2. The _____ _____ _____ family is made up of six metals (beryllium, magnesium, calcium, strontium, barium, and radium).
3. The members of the _____ series are all radioactive.
4. The _____ family is given its name because of the symbols of the lightest elements in each column of the family: boron, carbon, nitrogen, and oxygen.
5. The _____ are a family of poisonous nonmetals.
6. All of the members of the _____ _____ family are colorless, tasteless, and odorless gases.
7. All 15 members of the _____ series of elements are soft, silvery metals.
8. All of the metals of the _____ _____ family are soft, silvery-white metals with low melting points.

Uses of Elements
Directions: Study each of the pictures below. Write the name of one element that is used in making the object in each picture.

1.
2.
3.
4.

1. _____
2. _____
3. _____
4. _____

Element Symbols
Directions: Write the symbol for each element below.

Name	Symbol
1. Iron	_____
2. Silver	_____
3. Potassium	_____
4. Gold	_____
5. Sodium	_____
6. Helium	_____
7. Hydrogen	_____

Name: _____   Date: _____

PERIODIC LAW
Investigate

Activity #1–Elements
Directions: Use a Periodic Table to give the following information about each of the elements listed below.

Oxygen
1. Atomic Number _____
2. Symbol _____
3. Family Number _____
4. Family Name _____
5. Solid, Liquid, or Gas _____
6. Metal, Nonmetal, or Metalloid _____
7. Natural or Manmade _____
8. Radioactive or Stable _____

Uranium
9. Atomic Number _____
10. Symbol _____
11. Family Number _____
12. Family Name _____
13. Solid, Liquid, or Gas _____
14. Metal, Nonmetal, or Metalloid _____
15. Natural or Manmade _____
16. Radioactive or Stable _____

Activity #2–Element Symbols
Use a Periodic Table to fill in the blanks below.

Directions: Write the symbol in the space.
1. Magnesium _____   2. Lead _____
3. Chlorine _____   4. Carbon _____
5. Oxygen _____   6. Sulfur _____
7. Silicon _____   8. Copper _____
9. Iodine _____   10. Nickel _____

Directions: Write the name in the space.
11. Ag _____
12. Al _____
13. Au _____
14. C _____
15. Ca _____
16. P _____
17. Hg _____
18. Fe _____
19. H _____
20. He _____

Activity #3–Families
Directions: Use a Periodic Table to fill in the blanks below. In the space provided, write the name of the family to which each element belongs.
1. Silver _____
2. Helium _____
3. Arsenic _____
4. Sodium _____
5. Chlorine _____
6. Nitrogen _____
7. Calcium _____

Directions: Give one use for each of the following elements.
8. Aluminum _____
9. Iodine _____
10. Terbium _____
11. Uranium _____
12. Beryllium _____

UNIT 2: SCIENTIFIC LAWS
Lesson 2: Newton's Laws of Motion

Laws of Motion

Newton's Laws of Motion explain the relationship between force and motion.

The Act of Moving

Motion is the act of moving from one place to another. Isaac Newton is the English scientist who stated the three Laws of Motion in 1687. The Laws were named after him.

- **The First Law (Law of Inertia)** states an object at rest stays at rest until acted upon by another force; it stays in motion in a straight line at a constant speed until acted upon by another force. (If a ball is not moving, it will stay that way until some force makes it move.)

- **The Second Law (Law of Acceleration)** states that acceleration produced by a force on a body is directly proportional to the magnitude of the net force, is in the same direction as the force, and is inversely proportional to the mass of the body. (If two bike riders pedal with the same force, the rider moving less mass accelerates faster.)

- **The Third Law (Law of Action and Reaction)** states that for every action there is an equal and opposite reaction. (A boy jumps on a trampoline. The action force is the boy pushing down on the trampoline. The reaction force is the trampoline pushing up on the boy.)

My three laws apply to anything that moves.

Sir Isaac Newton (1642–1727), is responsible for developing the Laws of Motion.

Newton and You

Newton's Laws of Motion explain how most sports happen, including skateboarding, skiing, and dirt bike racing.

NEWTON'S LAWS OF MOTION
Knowledge Builder

First Law of Motion: The Law of Inertia

First Law

Objects do not start or stop by themselves. An object at rest, or not moving, tends to stay at rest. A moving object tends to keep moving in a straight line until it is affected by a force to stop it. A **force** is a push or a pull.

Push your empty desk. It moves, and then stops. Why? **Friction**. Frictional forces act in the direction opposite to your push. If you put wheels under your desk legs, it moves farther with the same push because of less friction. If there were no friction or other force (like a wall at the other side of the room) acting against your push force, the desk would move forever. This tendency to keep moving is called **inertia**, and it depends on the **mass** of the object. A chair will move faster with the same push than the desk. The desk has more mass, so it takes more force to move the desk.

Mass

Mass is a measurement of the amount of matter (stuff) in an object. The greater the mass of an object, the more inertia it has.

Example: The mass of a bowling ball is greater than the mass of a tennis ball.

Friction

Friction is a force that resists motion. Frictional forces are forces that act in a direction opposite to motion. Friction occurs when one object slides over another object. The larger the mass of an object, the greater the friction.

Example: A heavy box is difficult to push across a carpeted floor. It resists the sliding movement.

Inertia

Another way to state Newton's First Law of Motion is that all objects have inertia. **Inertia** is the tendency of objects to resist a change in their state of motion. The greater an object's mass, the greater its inertia and the larger the force needed to overcome the inertia.

Example: A car drives next to a semi truck, both traveling at 65 miles per hour. If both drivers slam on the brakes at the same time, the car will stop in a relatively short distance while the semi truck will travel much further before it stops.

Force

Force is a push or a pull. Force appears in pairs and can be either balanced or unbalanced. Balanced forces produce no change in the motion of an object. They are equal in size and opposite in direction. Unbalanced forces produce a change in the motion of an object in the direction of the greatest force.

Example: When the forces are balanced in a game of tug of war, the flag in the center of the rope will not move. When the forces are unbalanced, the flag in the center of the rope will move in the direction of the greatest force.

NEWTON'S LAWS OF MOTION
Knowledge Builder

Second Law of Motion: The Law of Acceleration

Second Law

The **Second Law** explains the relationship between acceleration, mass, and force. **Acceleration** depends on the **mass** of an object and the **force** pushing or pulling the object.

- Large mass, small acceleration
- Small mass, large acceleration
- Large force, large acceleration
- Small force, small acceleration

Acceleration

Acceleration is any change in the speed or direction of an object.

Example: Throughout a roller-coaster ride, speed and direction change.

Mass

Mass is a measurement of the amount of matter (stuff) in an object.

Example: The mass of an elephant is greater than the mass of a mouse.

Force

Force is a push or a pull.

Example: Pushing a shopping cart

A Newton

The unit for measuring force, honoring Sir Isaac Newton, is called a **newton**, abbreviated **N**. In the metric system, one newton of force is needed to accelerate one kilogram of mass at the rate of one meter per second per second ($1N = 1kg \cdot m/sec/sec$).

$F = m \times a$

The relationship between acceleration, mass, and force can be written as an equation.

Force = mass x acceleration
or   F = m x a

The equation can be rearranged to find acceleration or mass. The circle shows you how to do this:

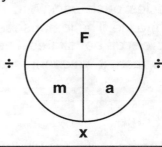

Divide **F** by **m** to find acceleration.
Divide **F** by **a** to find mass.
Multiple **a** by **m** to find force.

Example: If you exert a force of 10 N on a 5-kg object, what will its acceleration be?

Problem: $a = \dfrac{10\ N}{5\ kg}$

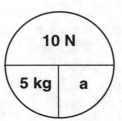

Answer: $a = 2\ m/s/s$

NEWTON'S LAWS OF MOTION
Knowledge Builder

Third Law of Motion: The Law of Action and Reaction

Newton's Third Law

Newton discovered that forces never occur alone. They occur in pairs. One force always produces another force. Newton called the first force the action. He called the second force the reaction. His discoveries became the **Third Law of Motion**. For every action, there is an equal and opposite reaction.

Example: An ice skater moves ahead on slippery ice. Her skates cut into the ice. Her leg muscles push backward (action force) against the ice. The ice pushes forward (reaction force) on her skates. The result is the greater speed at which the skater moves.

Balanced and Unbalanced Forces

Force is a push or a pull. Force appears in pairs and can be either balanced or unbalanced. **Balanced forces** produce **no change** in the motion of an object. They are equal in size and opposite in direction. **Unbalanced forces** produce a **change** in the motion of an object in the direction of the greatest force.

Example: Two people are pushing (force) a box toward each other at opposite ends. The box will not move because of the balanced force.

Example: Two people are pushing (force) a box toward one person. The box will move because the forces are unbalanced.

Action Force

A force (push or pull) that causes another equal but opposite force is called an **action force**.

Example: When you sit on a stool, you push down on the seat. Your push is the action force. The reaction force is the stool pushing up on you. The direction of your force is downward. The direction of the stool's force is upward. If the force of the stool did not exist, you would fall to the floor. It takes two objects to make opposing forces. You and the stool form an action and reaction pair.

Reaction Force

A force (push or pull) caused by an action force is a **reaction force**.

Example: If you kick a soccer ball, you will feel an impact when your foot hits the ball. The impact is the ball pushing back on your foot. In the picture, the action force is the boy's kick on the soccer ball. The reaction force is the impact of the ball on the boy's foot.

Name: _____ Date: _____

NEWTON'S LAWS OF MOTION
Understanding Formulas

> ***Formula:*** **Force = mass x acceleration**
> **or F = m x a**

1. A boy pulls on a 50-kg wagon with a constant force of 400 newtons. What is the wagon's acceleration? Show your work below.

   Formula: Force = mass x acceleration
   F = m x a

   Problem: $a = \dfrac{400 \text{ N}}{50 \text{ kg}}$

   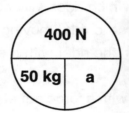

   Answer: _____

2. A car has a mass of 3,000 kg and accelerates at 6 m/s/s. The force acting on the car is _____ m/s/s. Show your work below.

   Formula: Force = mass x acceleration
   F = m x a

   Problem:
   F = 3,000 kg x 6 m/s/s

   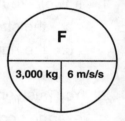

   Answer: _____

3. A force of 4,500 N acts on a car. The acceleration of the car is 3 m/s/s. What is the mass of the car? Show your work below.

   Formula: Force = mass x acceleration
   F = m x a

   Problem: $m = \dfrac{4,500 \text{ N}}{3 \text{ m/s/s}}$

   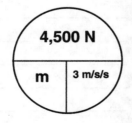

   Answer: _____

4. A baseball has a mass of 0.20 kg. What is the force on the ball if its acceleration is 60 m/s/s? Show your work below.

   Formula: Force = mass x acceleration
   F = m x a

   Problem:
   F = 0.20 kg x 60 m/s/s

   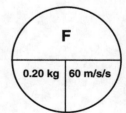

   Answer: _____

25

Name: _____ Date: _____

NEWTON'S LAWS OF MOTION
Apply

Matching

_____ 1. mass
_____ 2. force
_____ 3. acceleration
_____ 4. inertia
_____ 5. friction

a. any change in the speed or direction of an object
b. the tendency of objects to resist a change in their state of motion
c. a measurement of the amount of matter in an object
d. a force that resists motion
e. a push or pull

Multiple Choice

1. If two bike riders pedal with the same force, which rider will accelerate faster?

   a. the strongest rider
   b. the rider moving the most mass
   c. the rider moving the least mass
   d. the rider with the best bike

2. You push on a wall and the wall pushes back with a force equal in strength to the force you exerted according to _____.

   a. Newton's First Law of Motion
   b. Newton's Second Law of Motion
   c. Newton's Third Law of Motion
   d. Newton's Fourth Law of Motion

Work It Out

A tennis ball has a mass of 0.10 kg. What is the force on the ball if its acceleration is 50 m/s/s? Show your work below.

Answer: _____

Constructed Response

Observe the speed boat in the picture. Identify the action and reaction forces.

_____
_____
_____
_____
_____
_____
_____

Name: _____   Date: _____

NEWTON'S LAWS OF MOTION
Investigate

Activity #1—First Law of Motion

Materials: 5 checkers (with smooth sides), 1 ruler
Procedure:
Step #1:   Stack the checkers to make a tower.
Step #2:   Lay the ruler flat on the table. Swing the ruler sideways quickly so that you only hit the bottom checker.
Step #3:   Stack the checkers again. Try removing the checkers one by one without knocking over the tower.

Observations: Record your observations on your own paper.
Conclusions: Record your conclusions on your own paper.

Activity #2—Second Law of Motion

Materials: grooved ruler, 1″ block, 1 marble, 1 small ball bearing, 1 large ball bearing, meter stick
Procedure:
Step #1:   Place the block on the floor. Place one end of the ruler on the block and the other on the floor.
Step #2:   Place the marble at the top of the ramp and release. Measure the distance the marble travels. Record the measurement in the data table below.
Step #3:   Repeat Step #2 with the ball bearings.

Results:

Distance of Marble	Distance of Small Bearing	Distance of Large Bearing

Conclusions: Record your conclusions on your own paper.

Activity #3—Third Law of Motion

Materials: balloon, a plastic straw, tape, and a 5-meter length of fishing line
Procedure:
Step #1:   Thread the fishing line through the straw.
Step #2:   Attach one end of the fishing line to the top of a wall and hold the other in one hand.
Step #3:   Blow up the balloon and pinch off the mouth. Tape the straw to the balloon while still holding the balloon closed.
Step #4:   Holding the fishing line taut, release the balloon.

Observations: Record your observations on your own paper.
Conclusions: Record your conclusions on your own paper.

Name: _____ Date: _____

NEWTON'S LAWS OF MOTION
Inquiry Lab

Purpose: Determine if mass affects the speed of a toy car rolling down a ramp.

Hypothesis: Mass affects/doesn't affect (circle one) the speed of a toy car rolling down a ramp.

Materials:

toy car	stopwatch
triple beam-balance	meter stick
3 books	3 washers
ramp (at least 1 meter long)	tape

Procedure:

Step 1: Find the mass of the car and record it in the data table below.

Step 2: Stack the three books on the floor. Place one end of the ramp on the books and the other on the floor.

Step 3: Place the rear wheels of the car at the top end of the ramp.

Step 4: Release the car as you start the stopwatch.

Step 5: Stop timing when the front of the car gets to the bottom of the ramp. Record the time in the data table. Repeat steps 3–5 two more times. Calculate the average speed of your car and record in the data table below.

Step 6: Tape the washers on top of the car. Find the mass and record in the data table below.

Step 7: Repeat steps 3–5.

Results:

	Car (No Washers)			Car (3 Washers)		
Trial #	Mass (g)	Distance (cm)	Time (s)	Mass (g)	Distance (cm)	Time (s)
#1						
#2						
#3						
Average speed:				Average speed:		

Conclusion: _____

_____

_____

_____

_____

_____

UNIT 2: SCIENTIFIC LAWS
Lesson 3: Law of Conservation of Momentum

The Law of Conservation of Momentum

The Law of Conservation of Momentum states that the total momentum of objects that collide with each other is the same before and after the collision.

Measuring Momentum

The **momentum** of an object is a measure of how hard it is to stop that object. It depends on the object's mass and velocity (speed). Mass is measured in kilograms and velocity in meters per second, so momentum is measured in kg·m/sec.

Formula: **Momentum (p) equals mass (m) times velocity (v)**
p = mv

This law took a lot of great thinkers!

Great Thinkers

The concept of momentum was developed over time by a number of great thinkers.

- In 1027, Ibn Sina, a Persian, noted a relation between the weight and velocity of a moving body in his book, *The Book of Healing*.

Ibn Sina

- This idea was later adopted and further refined by the European philosophers Peter Olivi (1248–1298) and Jean Buridan (1300–1358).

- René Descartes (1596–1650), a French philosopher, developed the first formal definitions and measurement of momentum.

René Descartes

- Sir Isaac Newton (1643–1727), an English physicist, mathematician, and astronomer, stated more fully and with better mathematics what was already known about the concept of momentum. Newton used the Third Law of Motion to develop the Law of Conservation of Momentum.

Sir Isaac Newton

LAW OF CONSERVATION OF MOMENTUM
Knowledge Builder

Momentum

The faster an object moves, the harder it is to stop. Just as increasing the mass of an object makes it harder to stop, so does increasing the **velocity**, or speed, of the object. **Momentum** of an object is a measure of how hard it is to stop the object, and it depends on the object's mass and velocity.

Example:

- Bullets have small masses, but they can create great damage because their velocity is so high.

Collisions

When objects collide, some of the momentum is transferred.

Example:

- When a bowling ball hits the pins, some of its momentum is transferred to the pins. The ball slows down, and the pins start moving as their momentum increases.

Properties of Matter

Objects have many properties. One important property of an object is its mass. The **mass** of an object is the amount of matter in the object. Objects with more mass weigh more than objects with less mass. A bowling ball has more mass than a beach ball, so it weighs more than the beach ball. However, the size of an object is not the same as the mass of the object. The beach ball is larger than the bowling ball, but the bowling ball has more mass.

The more mass an object has, the harder it is to change its motion. This tendency of an object to resist change in its motion is called **inertia**. Objects with more mass have more inertia.

Mass is measured in kilograms and velocity in meters per second, so momentum is measured in kg·m/sec.

Conservation of Momentum

According to the Law of Conservation of Momentum, the total momentum of objects that collide is the same before and after the collision.

Example:

If you have ever shot marbles, you know that when one marble hits another marble, the motions of both marbles change.

- The first marble slows down and may change directions, so its momentum decreases.
- The second marble starts moving, so its momentum increases. Momentum is transferred from the first marble to the second marble.

Explanation:

During the collision, the momentum lost by the first marble was gained by the other marble. The total momentum of the two marbles was the same just before and just after the collision.

Name: _____ Date: _____

LAW OF CONSERVATION OF MOMENTUM
Understanding Formulas

Formula: Momentum (p) equals mass (m) times velocity (v)
or p = mv

The relationship between momentum, mass, and velocity can be written as an equation.

Momentum (p) equals mass (m) times velocity (v) or
p = mv

The equation can be rearranged to find mass or velocity. The circle shows you how to do this:

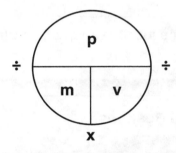

Divide **p** by **m** to find velocity.
Divide **p** by **v** to find mass.
Multiply **m** by **v** to find momentum.

Example: What is the momentum of a 15-kg bicycle traveling 3 m/s?

Problem: p = 15 x 3

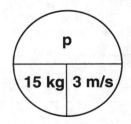

Answer: p = 45 kg·m/s

1. What is the velocity of a 3-kg ball that has a momentum of 15 kg·m/s? Show your work below.

Formula: p = mv

Problem: $v = \dfrac{15 \text{ kg·m/s}}{3 \text{ kg}}$

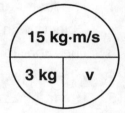

Answer: _____

2. A 160-kg lineman picks up a fumble and heads toward the goal line. He hits another player to make a touchdown. The player he hits is moving at 4 meters/sec. What is the lineman's momentum? Show your work below.

Formula: p = mv

Problem: p = 160 kg x 4 m/s

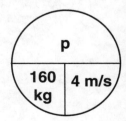

Answer: _____

Name: _____ Date: _____

LAW OF CONSERVATION OF MOMENTUM
Apply

Matching

_____ 1. velocity
_____ 2. momentum
_____ 3. mass
_____ 4. inertia
_____ 5. Law of Conservation
          of Momentum

a. the amount of matter in an object
b. total momentum of objects that collide with each other
    is the same before and after the collision
c. tendency of an object to resist change in its motion
d. speed of an object
e. a measure of how hard it is to stop an object

Fill in the Blanks

1. The faster an object moves, the harder it is to _____.
2. Objects with more mass _____ more than objects with less mass.
3. The more mass an object has, the harder it is to change its _____.
4. When objects collide, some of the momentum is _____.
5. The total _____ of two objects is the same just before and just after a collision.

Work It Out

A 126-kg lineman picks up a fumble and heads toward the goal line. He hits another player to make a touchdown. The player he hits is moving at 3 meters/sec. What is the lineman's momentum? Show your work.

Answer: _____

Constructed Response

Which object has more momentum: a taxi traveling 11 km/h or a baseball pitched at 150 km/h? Explain your answer.

_____
_____
_____
_____
_____
_____

Name: _____ Date: _____

LAW OF CONSERVATION OF MOMENTUM
Investigate

Activity #1—Marbles

Materials: 2 meter sticks   4 marbles

Procedure:
Step #1: Tape the 2 meter sticks parallel to each other 1 cm apart.
Step #2: Place 3 marbles in the middle of the meter sticks about 2 cm apart.
Step #3: Start a fourth marble rolling toward the other marbles.

Observations:

_____

_____

Conclusion:

How did this activity demonstrate the Law of Conservation of Momentum?

_____

_____

_____

Activity #2—Bouncing Balls

Materials: tennis ball   basketball

Procedure:
Step #1: Hold the small ball on top of the larger ball at a comfortable height.
Step #2: Release the balls at the same time. (If the balls are aligned correctly, the large ball should stop dead on the floor and the small ball should hit the ceiling.)

Observations:

_____

_____

Conclusion:

How did this activity demonstrate the Law of Conservation of Momentum?

_____

_____

_____

UNIT 2: SCIENTIFIC LAWS
Lesson 4: Law of Universal Gravitation

Universal Gravitation

The **Law of Universal Gravitation** states that all objects attract each other in proportion to their masses and how far apart they are.

Gravitational Attraction

Sir Isaac Newton developed the Law of Universal Gravitation. According to Newton's law, every object in the universe attracts every other object. He called the force of attraction between objects **gravitational attraction**, also known as **gravity**. The amount of gravitational attraction between objects depends on how much mass the objects have and how far apart the objects are.

Objects that are close together attract each other more than objects that are farther apart.

Weight and Mass

Weight and mass are different. **Mass** is a measurement of the amount of matter (stuff) in an object. **Weight** is the measurement of the pull of gravity on an object. Every time you weigh yourself on a scale, you are measuring the pull of the Earth's gravity. The mass of an object doesn't change when an object moves from place to place but weight does.

Sir Isaac Newton (1642–1727), a mathematician and physicist, is responsible for the Law of Universal Gravitation.

Why do objects always fall down instead of up?

Newton and the Apple

Newton was always thinking about why things happen. One story tells how one day he was sitting in his garden. While there, he saw an apple fall from a tree. He wondered, "Why did the apple fall down? Why didn't it fall up?" He thought that it was because of some force, a power, or energy.

It took Newton many years before he could explain the force. In 1687, Newton outlined his Law of Gravity in his book *Philosophiæ Naturalis Principia Mathematica* (referred to as the *Principia*).

LAW OF UNIVERSAL GRAVITATION
Knowledge Builder

Gravitational Force

Falling Objects

Drop a baseball and a bowling ball from the same height, and you will discover they will hit the ground at the same time. Drop them from the roof, and they will not only hit the ground at the same time, but also will be moving faster. All falling objects accelerate at the same rate—a fact not scientifically demonstrated until the late 1500s when Galileo dropped two cannonballs of different sizes from the top of the Leaning Tower of Pisa in Italy.

If an object accelerates, a force must be acting on it. The force acting on falling objects is the **force of gravity**. Abbreviated "g," gravity accelerates falling objects at the rate of 9.8 m/sec/sec. After one second, an object will be falling at 9.8 m/sec, but after two seconds, it will be falling at the rate of 2 x 9.8 m/sec or 19.6 m/sec. You can do the math. Even a marble becomes a dangerous missile when dropped from a great height.

In the examples above, we have neglected a force that becomes important for light objects (or even fairly heavy objects that have to fall a long way). This is the upward force of air molecules called air resistance. When the upward force of **air resistance** equals the force of gravity, a falling object stops accelerating and reaches a constant **terminal velocity**. The terminal velocity for skydivers is about 190 km/h.

The Force of Gravity

Sir Isaac Newton realized that the force of gravity influenced not only earthly objects, but those in the heavens, too, like the moon. His Law of Universal Gravitation states that all objects attract each other in proportion to their masses and how far apart they are. **Gravitational force = $G(M_1 M_2)/r^2$**, where **G** is a constant (and very small number), **M_1** and **M_2** are two masses, and **r** is the distance between them.

Weight

The weight of an object is the force exerted by the force of gravity acting on its mass. **Weight = mass x force of gravity**. *An object's mass is always the same* (whether on Earth or in a galaxy far, far away), *but an object's weight depends on the large mass it is near.*

Name: _____   Date: _____

LAW OF UNIVERSAL GRAVITATION
Understanding Formulas

Formula: Weight = mass x force of gravity
or W = m x g

Gravitational Pull on Earth

On the earth, the force of gravity is 9.81 newtons per kg. This means that for every kg of mass, you would have a force downwards (your weight) of approximately 10 N.

Formula:

Weight = mass x force of gravity
W = mg
W = m x 9.81N/kg

In the formula above, one element of the formula never changes when solving a problem. That is the number 9.81. In working with formulas, you will often find there is an element that always represents the same number. The number in a formula that always is the same is called the **constant**.

Example: If an object has a mass of 10 kilograms, what is its weight near the surface of the Earth?

Problem: W = 10 kg x 9.81N/kg

Answer: W = 98.1 N/kg

1. What is the weight of a 180-kg football player? Show your work below.

Formula:
Weight = mass x force of gravity
W = m x g

Problem: W = 180 kg x 9.81 N/kg

Answer: _____

2. An astronaut with a mass of 85 kg is traveling to Mars. What is her weight on Earth before she leaves? Show your work below.

Answer: _____

Name: _____   Date: _____

LAW OF UNIVERSAL GRAVITATION
Understanding Formulas

Formula: **Distance = 4.9 meters x time²**
d = 4.9 x t²

Falling Objects

Gravity affects the distance an object will fall in a given period of time. Gravity also affects the speed of an object as the period of time passes.

An important formula for finding the distance an object will fall in a given amount of time is **d = 4.9t²**. This formula says that distance equals 4.9 meters multiplied by time squared. The letter "d" in the formula stands for distance. The letter "t" stands for time.

To square "t" (time) means that the number substituted in the formula for "t" is multiplied times itself. If "t" equals 2, then "t²" equals 2 x 2 or 4.

Formula: **distance = 4.9 x time² or d = 4.9t²**

In the formula above, one element of the formula never changes when solving problems. The number 4.9 is the constant in this formula.

Determine the Distance an Object Falls

When using the formula to determine the distance an objects falls, time is measured from the instant the object is dropped. Distance is measured downward from the point where the object dropped.

The chart below shows the distance a ball falls when dropped from the roof of a 122-meter tall building. The chart shows the time and formula for determining the distance the ball falls each second.

Complete the calculations for the chart.

Time Ball Falls	Formula			Distance Ball Falls
1. 1 second	d = 4.9t²	d = 4.9 x 1²	d = 4.9 x 1	d = 4.9
2. 2 seconds	d = 4.9t²	d = 4.9 x 2²	d = 4.9 x 4	d = 19.6
3. 3 seconds	d = 4.9t²	d = 4.9 x 3²	d = 4.9 x _____	d = _____
4. 4 seconds	d = 4.9t²	d = 4.9 x 4²	d = 4.9 x _____	d = _____
5. 5 seconds	d = 4.9t²	d = 4.9 x 5²	d = 4.9 x _____	d = _____

Name: _____   Date: _____

LAW OF UNIVERSAL GRAVITATION
Understanding Formulas

> ***Formula:* Speed = 9.8 meters x time**
> **s = 9.8t**

Falling Objects

    Gravity affects the distance an object will fall in a given period of time. Gravity also affects the speed of an object as the period of time passes.

    In determining speed or the acceleration rate of a falling object, meters per second is used rather than feet per second.

    The formula for the speed of a dropped ball in meters is:

Formula: speed = 9.8 meters x time
s = 9.8t

    In the formula above, one element of the formula never changes when solving a problem. The number 9.8 is the constant.

Speed

Complete the following problems to find the speed in meters of a ball dropped from a building. Show your work below each question. Use the formula to find the correct answer.

1. The ball's speed after two seconds is _____ meters per second.

2. The ball's speed after five seconds is _____ meters per seconds.

3. The ball's speed after eight seconds is _____ meters per seconds.

Name: _____ Date: _____

LAW OF UNIVERSAL GRAVITATION
Apply

Matching

_____ 1. mass

_____ 2. Law of Universal Gravitation

_____ 3. force of gravity

_____ 4. weight

_____ 5. constant

a. the force acting on falling objects

b. the measurement of the pull of gravity on an object

c. a measurement of the amount of matter in an object

d. number in a formula that is always the same

e. all objects attract each other in proportion to their masses and how far apart they are

---

Multiple Choice

1. Gravity accelerates falling objects at what rate?

   a. 9.81 N/g   b. $32t^2$ c. 9.8 m/sec/sec   d. 4.45 N

2. Newton outlined his law of gravity in his book, _____.

   a. *Gravity*

   b. *Principia*

   c. *Laws of Universal Gravity*

   d. *Gravitational Force*

Work It Out

What is the weight of an automobile with the mass of 850 kg? Show your work.

Answer: _____

Constructed Response

Explain why a person who weighs 120 pounds on Earth would weigh 316.8 pounds on Jupiter.

_____

_____

_____

_____

_____

_____

_____

_____

Name: _____   Date: _____

LAW OF UNIVERSAL GRAVITATION
Investigate

Activity #1—Gravity
Directions: The chart below shows the weight of an object on the moon and on other planets. Complete the chart by calculating your weight on the moon, Mars, and Jupiter. To find your weigh on the moon, take 0.17 times your weight. To find your weight on Mars, take 0.38 times your weight. To find your weigh on Jupiter, take 2.64 times your weight.

Planet	Earth	Moon	Mars	Jupiter
Object's Weight	120 lbs.	20.4 lbs.	45.6 lbs.	316.8 lbs.
Your Weight in pounds (lbs)				
Your Weight in newtons (N)				

Covert your weight in pounds to newtons. In the United States, the force of gravity is often given in pounds. Scientists write about the force of gravity in newtons. They use the letter N for the newton. A pound is 4.45 newtons. To convert pounds to newtons, take the weight in pounds and multiply times 4.45 newtons (100 pounds x 4.45 = 445 N.)

Activity #2—Egg Drop

Materials:
eggs   one piece of cardboard   1 meter of yarn   1 sheet of newspaper
2 1-meter pieces of masking tape   1 meter of string   10 drinking straws
5 rubber bands   plastic bags

Procedure:
Step #1: Select a surface of about 5 feet from which to drop your egg. Beneath that surface, place plastic bags on the floor.
Step #2: Use any materials from those available to create packaging around the egg that you think will protect the egg from breaking when it hits the surface. Your container may not be larger than 12 inches by 12 inches by 12 inches.
Step #3: Drop the egg within the packaging from 5 feet.
Step #4: Observe your results. Did the egg break? If so, then hypothesize why and create new packaging. If the egg did not break, then hypothesize why not.
Step #5: Continue with the experiment until you create packaging that protects the egg from breaking during the drop. This may take many different tries to get right, so don't worry if the egg breaks.

UNIT 2: SCIENTIFIC LAWS
Lesson 5: Law of Conservation of Matter

Law of Conservation of Matter

The **Law of Conservation of Matter** is also known as the Law of Conservation of Mass. It states that matter is not created or destroyed; it can only change form.

> Linking facts with experimentation, I have discovered the truth of matter.

Antoine-Laurent Lavoisier

Antoine-Laurent Lavoisier is considered the founder of modern chemistry because of his strict approach to research. Studying combustion, he was the first to identify two gases in the air, oxygen and azote (now called nitrogen). Lavoisier defined burning as the uniting of a substance with oxygen. He determined that although matter may change its form or shape, its mass remains the same. All the atoms present at the start of the reaction are also present at the end of the reaction. This is known as the Law of Conservation of Matter.

Antoine-Laurent Lavoisier (1743–1794), a French chemist, is considered the founding father of modern chemistry.

Release or Consume Energy

Chemical reactions happen all around us: when we light a campfire, start a scooter, eat lunch, or run track. A **chemical reaction** is the process by which substances form or break bonds, and in doing so, either release or consume energy.

Chemical Reaction

During an ordinary chemical change, there is no detectable increase or decrease in the quantity of matter.

Example: Burning candle

- The mass of the wick, wax that burned, and the oxygen that helped the flame before the reaction equals the mass of the smoke and the gases released after the reaction.

Chemical Equation

A **chemical equation** is the shorthand that scientists use to describe a chemical reaction.

Example: The reaction of hydrogen with oxygen to form water.

$$4H + O_2 \longrightarrow 2H_2O$$
reactants   **product**

The **reactants** (substances reacting) are written on the left side of an equation with an arrow pointing to the **products** (substances being formed) on the right side of the equation.

LAW OF CONSERVATION OF MATTER
Knowledge Builder

Chemical Reactions

Chemical Equations

A **chemical equation** is a shorthand way of describing a chemical reaction between two or more substances. The letters are the symbols that represent the element. A "+" sign means "combines with." An arrow points away from the reactants and toward the products. An arrow means "yields."

$$2Na \ + \ Cl_2 \longrightarrow 2NaCl$$ means sodium combines with chlorine to yield sodium chloride (salt).

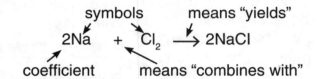

Look closely at the equation above. Notice the "2" in front of Na and NaCl. That 2 is called a **coefficient**. It is necessary to make this equation balanced. Matter is neither created nor destroyed in a chemical reaction. The same number of each kind of atom must be on both sides of a chemical equation. Because chlorine only exists as a molecule consisting of two chlorine atoms, it requires two atoms of sodium to yield two molecules of salt (NaCl).

Balance the Coefficient

Complete the following problems to balance the coefficient in the chemical equations. Remember, both sides of the equation must be balanced. Show your work below each question.

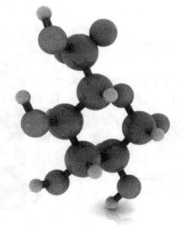

1. _____ H + _____ O_2 $\longrightarrow$ $4H_2O$

2. _____ Na + $6Cl_2$ $\longrightarrow$ $12NaCl$

3. $4C$ + _____ O_2 $\longrightarrow$ $4CO_2$

4. _____ Fe + _____ S $\longrightarrow$ $3FeS$

5. _____ Mg + $2O_2$ $\longrightarrow$ $4MgO$

Name: _____ Date: _____

LAW OF CONSERVATION OF MATTER
Apply

Matching

_____ 1. chemical reaction
_____ 2. Law of Conservation of Matter
_____ 3. reactants
_____ 4. products
_____ 5. Lavoisier
_____ 6. chemical equation

a. substances reacting
b. substances being formed
c. considered the founder of modern chemistry
d. matter is not created or destroyed; it can only change form
e. a shorthand way of describing a chemical reaction between two or more substances
f. the process by which substances form bonds (or break bonds) and, in doing so, either release or consume energy

Critical Thinking

From Lavoisier's work came the Law of Conservation of Matter. Why do you think people before Lavoisier's work thought matter could appear and disappear? Explain your answer.

_____
_____
_____
_____

Work It Out

Balance the coefficients in the following chemical equations. Show your work.

$$\_\_\_\_ \ H_2 + \_\_\_\_ \ Br_2 \longrightarrow 4HBr$$

Bonus: What is HBr the chemical formula for? Write your answer below.

_____
_____

Multiple Choice

1. During an ordinary chemical change, there is no detectable increase or decrease in the quantity of _____.

   a. wick   b. matter

   c. smoke   d. wax

2. A balanced chemical equation must have the same number of which of these on both sides of the equations?

   a. reactants   b. atoms

   c. molecules   d. compounds

Constructed Response

When wood burns, a small amount of ash is made. Why is the mass of the wood before the fire not equal to the mass of the ashes after the reaction?

_____
_____
_____
_____
_____

Name: _____   Date: _____

LAW OF CONSERVATION OF MATTER
Investigate

Activity #1—Change in Matter
Materials: Alka-Seltzer™ tablet, glass beaker, 250 mL water
Procedure:
Step #1: Pour 250 mL of water into a glass beaker.
Step #2: Drop an Alka-Seltzer™ tablet into the water.

Observations:

_____

Conclusion:

Why is it hard to prove the Law of Conservation of Matter when a gas is produced?

_____

_____

Activity #2—Chemical Reaction
Materials: 250 mL vinegar, 15 mL baking soda, two paper cups,
　　　　　　　large resealable plastic baggie, balance scale
Procedure:
Step #1: Pour 250 mL of vinegar in one paper cup.
Step #2: Place 15 mL baking soda in the second cup.
Step #3: Put both cups in the plastic bag.
　　　　　Caution: Do not spill the contents of either cup.
Step #4: Determine the mass of the cups and their contents and the plastic bag. Record your
　　　　　measurement in the data table below.
Step #5: Seal the plastic bag.
Step# 6: Without opening the bag, pour the vinegar into the cup of baking soda.
Step #7: Without opening the bag, measure and record the mass of the contents of the plastic
　　　　　bag. Take care not to break the seal of the plastic bag while weighing.

Initial Mass (g)	Final Mass (g)	Change in Mass (g)

Observation:

What happened when you poured the vinegar into the cup of baking soda?

_____

Conclusion:

What is conservation of matter and how does it relate to this exercise?

_____

_____

_____

UNIT 2: SCIENTIFIC LAWS
Lesson 6: Laws of Thermodynamics

Thermodynamics

The Laws of Thermodynamics apply to the way heat moves around in the universe. The study of heat and its transformation to mechanical energy is called **thermodynamics**.

Work

Energy is the ability to do work.

First Law of Thermodynamics

The **First Law of Thermodynamics** states that energy changes form and moves from place to place, but the total amount doesn't change.

Mechanical Energy

The energy an object has because of its motion or position is **mechanical energy**. There are two kinds of mechanical energy: kinetic and potential energy.

Second Law of Thermodynamics

The **Second Law of Thermodynamics** states that heat always moves from a hot place to a cold place.

James Prescott Joule

Heat is energy!

thought of a clever experiment that showed the amount of heat generated could be precisely connected to the mechanical energy of motion. He measured the rise in temperature of the water in a beaker caused by the rotation of a paddlewheel turned by a falling weight. He found that the same amount of mechanical energy always produced the same amount of heat. Heat was a form of energy, too!

When scientists carefully measured all the forms of energy (including heat) involved in any activity, they found the total amount of energy was always the same before and after, even though energy forms had changed. They discovered that energy is conserved—a fundamental scientific concept. This is usually stated as the **Law of Conservation of Energy**: energy can neither be created or destroyed.

Unfortunately, my discovery resulted in a weapon of mass destruction.

Albert Einstein made a discovery that modified the Law of Conservation of Energy in one important way. He found a relationship between mass and energy that is written as energy (e) = mass (m) x c² or ($e = mc^2$). The "c" stands for the speed of light, a huge number. Square that number and you get an even larger number. The equation means that a small amount of mass can be—under extraordinary conditions, like at the center of a star—converted to a HUGE amount of energy. (Nuclear bombs later demonstrated that on Earth.) So now the Law of Conservation of Energy is usually stated; energy can neither be created nor destroyed *by ordinary means*. The total amount of mass and energy before and after any event is always the same.

LAWS OF THERMODYNAMICS
Knowledge Builder

Thermodynamics focuses on how heat transfers. Such processes usually result in work being done.

First Law of Thermodynamics

The First Law of Thermodynamics is basically a restatement of the Law of Conservation of Energy as it applies to thermal (heat) energy.

Energy changes form and moves from place to place, but the total amount doesn't change.

Remember
- Energy can be stored.
- Energy can move from matter to matter.
- Energy can be transformed from one type of energy to another type of energy.

Basic Concepts
States of Matter
- gas
- solid
- liquid
- plasma

Phases
- condensation: gas to liquid
- freezing: liquid to solid
- melting: solid to liquid
- sublimation: solid to gas
- vaporization: liquid or solid to gas

Thermal Energy

Thermal energy is the energy related to the temperature of a substance.

Heat

Heat is the transfer of thermal energy between substances that are at different temperatures.

Second Law of Thermodynamics

The Second Law of Thermodynamics explains how heat moves. Since heat is energy, heat flows from warm objects to cold objects, thus spreading out.

Basic Concepts
- thermal contact: two substances can affect each other's temperature
- thermal equilibrium: two substances in thermal contact that no longer transfer heat
- thermal expansion: during thermal contact, a substance expands in volume as it gains heat
- conduction: heat flows through a heated solid
- convection: heated particles transfer heat to another substance
- radiation: heat is transferred through electromagnetic waves
- insulation: low-conduction material is used to prevent heat transfer

Thermal Conductors and Insulators

The **heat capacity** of a substance indicates the ease with which a substance heats up. A good heat (thermal) **conductor** would have a low heat capacity, indicating that a small amount of energy causes a large temperature change. A good heat (thermal) **insulator** would have a large heat capacity, indicating that much energy is needed for temperature change.

Name: _____   Date: _____

LAWS OF THERMODYNAMICS
Apply

Matching

_____ 1. thermal energy
_____ 2. heat
_____ 3. Second Law of
            Thermodynamics
_____ 4. mechanical energy
_____ 5. radiation

a. says that heat always moves from a hot place to a
    cold place
b. the energy related to the temperature of a substance
c. electromagnetic waves
d. transfer of thermal energy between substances that are
    at different temperatures
e. the energy an object has because of its motion or
    position

Fill in the Blanks

1. There are two kinds of mechanical energy: _____ and _____
    energy.
2. The Second Law of Thermodynamics explains how _____ moves.
3. The First Law of Thermodynamics is basically a restatement of the Law of
    _____ of Energy.
4. The _____ _____ of a substance indicates the ease with
    which a substance heats up.
5. Heat always moves from a _____ place to a _____ place.

Constructed Response

When a warm object is placed in cold water, does the object give off warmth or does it take on cold? Explain your answer.

_____

_____

_____

_____

_____

_____

_____

Complete the Chart
Directions: Write conduction, convection, or radiation for each example given.

	Example	Method of Transfer
1.	sun heating the earth	
2.	spoon becomes warm in a cup of hot soup	
3.	heating a pot of water on the stove	
4.	popping popcorn	
5.	lava lamp	

LAWS OF THERMODYNAMICS
Investigate

Activity #1—Rubber Band

Materials: rubber band

Procedure:

Step #1: Place a rubber band across your forehead and note its temperature.

Step #2: Remove the rubber band.

Step #3: Stretch the rubber band with both hands, then quickly place it across your forehead.

Observations: _____

_____

Conclusion: Why did the rubber band get hot? _____

_____

_____

_____

Activity #2—Heat Transfer

Materials: pot of water   hotplate   several ice cubes

Procedure:

Step #1: Heat the pot of water until boiling.

Step #2: Once the water comes to a steady boil, place several ice cubes into the pot.

Observations: _____

_____

_____

Conclusion: Why did the water stop boiling? _____

_____

_____

_____

UNIT 2: SCIENTIFIC LAWS
Lesson 7: Kepler's Laws of Planetary Motion

Kepler's Three Laws of Planetary Motion

- **First Law:** The orbit of a planet about the sun is an ellipse (an oval) with the sun at one focus.

- **Second Law:** A line joining a planet and the sun sweeps out equal areas in equal intervals of time. This means that a planet will move more quickly when it is closer to the sun and more slowly when it is farther away.

- **Third Law:** The square of the time it takes a planet to move around the sun is directly proportional to the cube of the average distance of the planet from the sun: (planet's year)^2 is proportional to (average distance from sun)^3.

> Planets orbit the sun in an oval shape.

Johannes Kepler (1571–1630) was a German mathematician, astronomer, and astrologer.

Nicolaus Copernicus

The sun, stars, and planets rise and set every day. It's easy for people to believe that these celestial objects are all small things orbiting around us and our world, the earth. And that's what people did think for most of human history.

Nicolaus Copernicus (1473–1543) proposed that the sun, not the earth, was the object around which all heavenly bodies in our solar system turned. His idea was not a guess. It explained age-old observations about the planetary motions in a simple and direct way.

Johannes Kepler (1571–1630), a mathematician among the next generation of scientists, was able to describe planetary motions more precisely with his three laws.

Isaac Newton

Kepler did not understand why his laws were correct. The physicist Sir Isaac Newton (1642–1727) was able to connect Kepler's laws to his own observations on force and motion and show that all masses, whether they were the size of planets or soccer balls or sand grains, were attracted to each other with a force that was inversely proportional to the square of the distance between them. In other words, two masses have the most attraction to each other at close range, and that attraction rapidly drops off with distance.

First Science-Fiction Story

Galileo sent Kepler a telescope to use in his study of the moon, stars, and planets. It is believed his observations inspired Kepler to write **Somnium**, a story about an imaginary trip to the moon, which may have been the first science-fiction story ever written.

KEPLER'S LAWS OF PLANETARY MOTION
Knowledge Builder

Planetary Motion

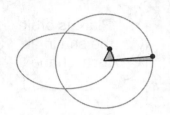

First Law: The orbit of a planet about the sun is an ellipse (an oval) with the sun at one focus.

Example: The center of the sun becomes the focus for a planet orbiting the sun.

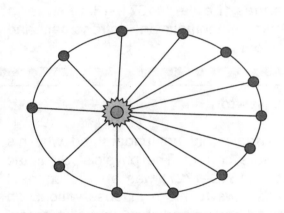

Second Law: A line joining a planet and the sun sweeps out equal areas in equal intervals of time.

Example: When a planet orbits the sun, the line joining it to the sun sweeps over equal areas in equal periods of time. Therefore, the speed of a planet changes, depending on its distance from the center of the sun. Speed is greatest at the point in the orbit closest to the sun and is slowest at the point farthest from the sun.

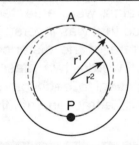

Third Law: The square of the time it takes a planet to move around the sun is directly proportional to the cube of the average distance of the planet from the sun.

Example: The farther a planet is from the sun, the longer it will take to complete an orbit, the greater the distance it will travel to complete an orbit, and the slower its average speed will be.

Name: _____   Date: _____

KEPLER'S LAWS OF PLANETARY MOTION
Apply

Matching

_____ 1. Nicolaus Copernicus   a. path

_____ 2. Johannes Kepler   b. center

_____ 3. focus   c. an oval

_____ 4. ellipse   d. described planetary motions
                                       more precisely with his three Laws

_____ 5. orbit   e. proposed that the sun, not the earth, was the object
                                       around which all heavenly bodies in our solar system
                                       turned

Fill in the Blanks

1. The physicist _____ _____ was able to connect Kepler's Laws to his own observations on force and motion.

2. Kepler wrote _____, a story about an imaginary trip to the moon, which was most likely the first science-fiction story ever written.

3. The speed of a planet changes, depending on its _____ from the center of the sun.

4. The center of the sun becomes the _____ for a planet orbiting the sun.

5. A planet will move more quickly when it is _____ to the sun and more _____ when it is farther away.

Multiple Choice

1. Kepler's three Laws explain _____.
   a. force and motion
   b. the relationship between mass and weight
   c. planetary motion
   d. the sun is center of solar system

2. What shape is the orbit of planets around the sun?
   a. circle   b. oval
   c. straight line   d. irregular shaped

Critical Thinking

Why was the work of Johannes Kepler important to astronomy?

_____

_____

_____

_____

_____

_____

_____

Name: _____   Date: _____

KEPLER'S LAWS OF PLANETARY MOTION
Investigate

Activity #1—Parts of an Ellipse

Materials: two push pins, piece of cardboard, a length of string, sharpened pencil, a blank piece of paper

Procedure:

Step #1: Place a piece of paper on a piece of cardboard and draw a horizontal line across the paper. Place two push pins on the line.

Step #2: Tie the ends of a piece of string together to make a loop wider than the distance between the pins.

Step #3: Put the loop over the pins and pull it tight with the writing end of a pencil in contact with the cardboard.

Step #4: Keeping tension on the loop, move the pencil around the pins. You will draw a figure like the one shown below.

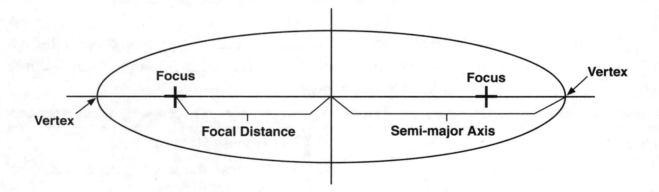

The two thumbtack holes are called the **focus points** of the ellipse. Each focus point is the same distance from the center of the ellipse. If the two focus points are far apart, the ellipse will be long. If they are close together, the ellipse will be almost round, like a circle.

The endpoints of the ellipse along its longest dimension are called the **vertices** of the ellipse. (Each of them by itself would be called a vertex.) The distance between the center of the ellipse and one of the vertices is called the **semi-major axis** of the ellipse. The distance from the center of the ellipse to one of the focus points is called the **focal distance**.

Directions: Label the focus points, vertices, and semi-major axis on your ellipse.

Name: _____   Date: _____

KEPLER'S LAWS OF PLANETARY MOTION
Investigate

Activity #2—Eccentricity

An ellipse property called the **eccentricity** measures how long and skinny or how round an ellipse is.

$$\text{eccentricity} = \frac{\text{focal distance}}{\text{semi-major axis}}$$

Example: $0.65 \text{ cm} = \dfrac{4 \text{ cm}}{6.2 \text{ cm}}$

The eccentricity can be a number between 0 and 1.

- If it is close to 1, the ellipse will be long and skinny.
- If it is close to 0, the ellipse will be almost a circle.

Directions: Calculate the eccentricities of the following ellipses by measuring the semi-major axis and the focal distance (in inches) and then dividing the focal distance by the semi-major axis. Round to the nearest hundredth.

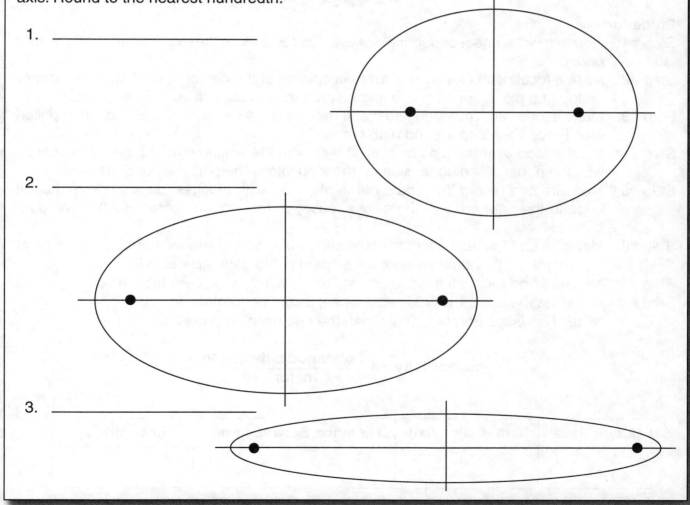

1. _____

2. _____

3. _____

Name: _____   Date: _____

KEPLER'S LAWS OF PLANETARY MOTION
Investigate

Activity #3—Eccentricity of an Ellipse

Materials: cardboard, string, metric ruler, two tacks, blank piece of paper, sharpened pencil

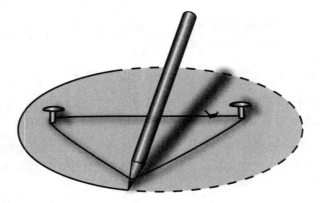

Procedure:

Step #1: Rotate a white sheet of paper sideways. Find and mark the exact center point of your paper.

Step #2: Mark a focal point exactly 5.0 cm to each side of the center point. Place your paper on top of a piece of cardboard and insert a thumbtack into each focal point.

Step #3: Make a loop with your string so that it measures 14 cm from end to end when pulled taut. Place your loop around both tacks.

Step #4: Put the loop over the pins and pull it tight with the writing end of a pencil in contact with the paper. Keeping tension on the loop, move the pencil around the pins.

Step #5: Measure and record the length of the major axis (the longest distance from the left edge to the right edge of the ellipse, passing through the center point) in the data table below.

Step #6: Measure and record the length of the semi-major axis (distance from the center point to either the left or right edge of the ellipse) in the data table below.

Step #7: Measure and record the distance between the foci in the data table below.

Step #8: Calculate the eccentricity of your ellipse, using the formula below.
Note: This is a different formula than the one used on page 53.

$$\text{eccentricity} = \frac{\text{distance between foci}}{\text{major axis}}$$

Major Axis	Semi-major Axis	Distance Between Foci	Eccentricity

UNIT 2: SCIENTIFIC LAWS
Lesson 8: Mendel's Laws of Genetics

Laws of Genetics
Mendel's First Law—Law of Segregation
- The two alleles for a trait must separate when gametes are formed.
- A parent randomly passes only one allele for each trait to each offspring.

Mendel's Second Law—Law of Independent Assortment
- The genes for different traits are inherited independently of each other.

Gregor Mendel (1822–1884) is known as the "father of genetics."

Traits

Gregor Mendel was the first person to describe how **traits** (characteristics passed down to an offspring by the parents) are inherited. He studied the inherited traits of pea plants. He noticed that genes always come in pairs. Every organism that reproduces sexually receives two genes for every trait. A trait may be **dominant** (stronger), and that trait will show up in the organism. If a trait is **recessive** (weaker), it will not show up in the organism unless the organism inherits two recessive genes.

Rule of Unit Factors
Each organism has two alleles for each trait.
- alleles: different forms of the same gene
- genes: located on chromosomes, they control how an organism develops

Rule of Dominance
- The trait that is observed in the offspring is the dominant trait.
- The trait that disappears in the offspring is the recessive trait.

Mendel's Pea Plants

Gregor Mendel, a monk, wanted to find out why animals and plants often looked alike over many generations. He began experimenting with short and tall pea plants. He chose pollen from a group of pea plants that had been short for many generations. He then took pollen from different pea plants that had been tall for many generations. He placed the pollen from the short plants into the flowers of tall plants. Then, he placed the pollen from the tall plants into the flowers of the short plants. This is known as **cross-pollination**.

Mendel found that the first generation of cross-pollinated plants were all tall. He then planted seeds from these plants. These seeds were the second generation of cross-pollinated pea plants. When these seeds produced pea plants, not all of them were tall. Three out of four of the plants were tall, but one out of four was short. Mendel knew there must be a reason why most plants were tall but others were short. Mendel had discovered how genes work. It was the plants' genes that made some plants tall and some short.

MENDEL'S LAWS OF GENETICS
Knowledge Builder

Heredity

Punnett Squares

Scientists use a **Punnett square**, designed by Reginald Punnett, to predict all possible gene combinations for the offspring of two parents. The Punnett square consists of four boxes inside a square. Each box represents a possible gene combination. The parent's genes are placed outside the square.

Example: The Punnett square below shows the cross between two tall pea plants. Each parent plant has one tall gene and one short gene. **T** = tall gene (dominant trait) and **t** = short gene (recessive trait).

Father's Genes

	T	t
T	TT (Tall)	Tt (Tall)
t	Tt (Tall)	tt (Short)

(Mother's Genes)

Look at the Punnett square above. The genetic makeup of an organism is its **genotype**. The genotype of the mother is **Tt**, and the genotype of the father is **Tt**. They each have a tall gene and a short gene, but because the tall gene is dominant, both plants appear tall. There are three possible genotypes for the offspring: **TT**, **Tt**, and **tt**. Using the Punnett square, scientists can predict that 75%, or 3⁄4, of the offspring will be tall plants. Only a plant that inherits two short genes (**tt**) will be short.

Heredity

Heredity explains why family members often look alike. It also explains how physical characteristics are passed from parents to children in families.

To understand heredity, one must learn about genes. There are thousands of cells in our body. Genes are found in the body cells. Each of us has 46 chromosomes in every cell of our body. **Chromosomes** are long strings of DNA found in cells. **DNA** is like a messenger. It tells the chromosomes the traits that each of us will inherit. Human **genes** are arranged as 23 pairs on the chromosomes. Each pair has a gene from the father and a gene from the mother. Therefore, each of us gets one-half of our genes from each parent. Genes give us hair color, eye color, and height. The things that we inherit are called **traits**. Each of us may also inherit traits such as color blindness and certain diseases.

Name: _____   Date: _____

MENDEL'S LAWS OF GENETICS
Apply

Matching

_____ 1. Punnett square   a. weaker trait
_____ 2. genes   b. contain DNA and are located on the chromosomes
_____ 3. inherited traits   c. stronger trait
_____ 4. dominant trait   d. characteristics passed down to an offspring by the
_____ 5. recessive trait   parents
                                e. used to predict all possible gene combinations for
                                   the offspring of two parents

---

Constructed Response

1. What is heredity? _____

   _____

2. What impact did Mendel's experiments with pea plants have on science?

   _____

   _____

   _____

Work It Out

Directions: Complete the Punnett square for hair type. Curly hair (**DD**) is dominant to straight hair (**dd**). The mother has curly hair, and her genotype is **DD**. The father has straight hair, and his genotype is **dd**.

1. What are the possible genotypes for hair type for their children? _____

2. What percent or fraction of their children will have curly hair? _____

Critical Thinking

What makes each person a unique individual?

_____

_____

_____

_____

_____

_____

_____

_____

Name: _____ Date: _____

MENDEL'S LAWS OF GENETICS
Investigate

Directions: Your genes (units in the chromosomes that contain your dominant and recessive traits) have been inherited from your parents. Below is a fun list of some common Mendelian traits. Do you have these traits? Which parent also has these traits? Complete the chart with your parents.

Mendelian Trait **D** = Dominant trait; **r** = Recessive trait	**You**	**Mother**	**Father**
Tongue Folding (**r**): ability to fold the tip of your tongue back upon the main body of the tongue without using your teeth	*Yes/No*	*Yes/No*	*Yes/No*
Detached Earlobes (**D**): earlobes not directly attached to your head; free-hanging	*Yes/No*	*Yes/No*	*Yes/No*
Attached Earlobes (**r**): earlobes directly attached to the head	*Yes/No*	*Yes/No*	*Yes/No*
Darwin's Tubercle (**D**): bump of cartilage on outer rim of ear	*Yes/No*	*Yes/No*	*Yes/No*
Hitchhiker's Thumb (**D**): thumb, when up in hitchhiking position, can bend backwards at a sharp angle (50% or more)	*Yes/No*	*Yes/No*	*Yes/No*
Dimples (**D**): natural smile produces dimples in one or both cheeks or a dimple in the center of the chin	*Yes/No*	*Yes/No*	*Yes/No*
Widow's Peak (**D**): pull hair off your forehead; hairline comes to a point in the middle of forehead	*Yes/No*	*Yes/No*	*Yes/No*
Bent little finger (**D**): little finger curves in toward other fingers	*Yes/No*	*Yes/No*	*Yes/No*
Webbing (**D**): spread fingers apart; grasp a thumbful of skin	*Yes/No*	*Yes/No*	*Yes/No*
Freckles (**D**): circular pattern of skin coloration	*Yes/No*	*Yes/No*	*Yes/No*
Whorl: The way the hair on the crown of your head turns—clockwise (**D**); counterclockwise (**r**)	*Yes/No*	*Yes/No*	*Yes/No*
Second toe longest (**D**): second toe is longer than the big toe	*Yes/No*	*Yes/No*	*Yes/No*

Conclusion: _____

_____

_____

_____

UNIT 3: SCIENTIFIC PRINCIPLES
Lesson 1: Archimedes' Principle

Archimedes' Principle

A body immersed in a fluid experiences a buoyant force equal to the weight of the fluid it displaces.

Archimedes

Archimedes discovered a method for finding the volume of an object with an irregular shape. King Hiero of Syracuse presented Archimedes with a problem. The king asked Archimedes to determine if his new crown was made of solid gold or whether the goldsmith had added silver. Archimedes was asked to solve the problem without damaging the crown.

One day, while getting into his bath, Archimedes observed water spilling over the sides of the tub. He recognized that there was a relationship between the amount of water that had run over the edge of the bath and the weight of his body. Archimedes immediately realized he had discovered why some objects float and some sink! He was so happy with this insight that he ran naked down the street yelling "Eureka! Eureka!" (The Greek word for "I have found it!")

He used this information to determine if the crown was made of pure gold. Archimedes compared how much water the crown displaced when it was submerged to the amount of water displaced by an equal volume of gold.

Eureka! Eureka!

Archimedes (287 B.C. to 212 B.C.) was a Greek mathematician and engineer.

How It Works

Archimedes' Principle
The buoyant force is equal to the weight of the displaced water.

3 lbs

3 lbs of water

- An object will sink if the weight of the water displaced is less than the weight of the object.
- An object will float if the weight of the water displaced is equal to the weight of the object.

Why Ships Float

A lump of steel will sink because it is unable to displace (push aside) water that equals its weight. However, steel of the same weight shaped as a bowl will float. This is because the weight gets distributed over a larger area, and the steel displaces water equal to its weight. A ship floats because its total weight is exactly equal to the weight of the water it displaces.

ARCHIMEDES' PRINCIPLE
Knowledge Builder

Sink or Float

Buoyancy

A **fluid** is a material, either liquid or gas, that can flow. All fluids exert pressure as their molecules move around and bump into the surface of other matter.

Buoyancy is the tendency of certain objects to float or rise in fluid. Buoyant force is the upward force exerted on an object that is immersed in a fluid. Buoyant force is caused by the difference in pressure within the fluid.

 All fluids, both liquid and gas, exert a buoyant force. As long as the buoyant force exerted on an object is less than the weight of the object, the object will sink.

 But, if the buoyant force is equal to the weight of the object, the object will float.

 And, if the buoyant force is greater than the weight of the object, the object will rise.

Density

Density is the relationship between the mass and volume of an object. The more closely packed the molecules, the greater the density of the object. By finding the mass and volume of the object, you can find the density mathematically. Density can be calculated by dividing the mass by volume.

Formula: Density $= \dfrac{\text{Mass}}{\text{Volume}}$ or $D = \dfrac{M}{V}$

Example: The mass of 1 milliliter of water is 1 gram.

The density of water is

$$D = \dfrac{1 \text{ gram}}{1 \text{ milliliter}} \quad \text{or} \quad D = 1 \text{ g/mL}$$

Knowing the relationship of mass to volume or density will help you determine whether or not an object will sink or float in a liquid. If the object's density is greater than the density of the liquid it is in, the object will sink. If the object's density is less than the density of the liquid it is in, the object will float.

Displacement

The volume of an irregular object, such as a rock, can be found by using a method called **displacement**. Water is added to a graduated cylinder and recorded. The rock is then added and the level of the water is recorded again. The difference between the first measurement and the second is the volume of the rock.

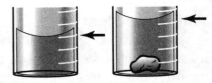

Name: _____   Date: _____

ARCHIMEDES' PRINCIPLE
Understanding Formulas

Formula: Density = $\dfrac{\text{Mass}}{\text{Volume}}$ or $D = \dfrac{M}{V}$

1. You are given a sample of a solid that has a mass of 10.0 g and a volume of 5.60 cm³. Will the solid float in liquid water, which has a density of 1.00 g/cm³? Show your work below.

Formula: Density = $\dfrac{\text{Mass}}{\text{Volume}}$ or $D = \dfrac{M}{V}$

Problem: $\dfrac{10.0 \text{ g}}{5.60 \text{ cm}^3}$

Answer: _____

2. A 6.20 cm³ sample of mercury has a mass of 102 g. Will it float in liquid water, which has a density of 1.00 g/cm³? Show your work below.

Formula: Density = $\dfrac{\text{Mass}}{\text{Volume}}$ or $D = \dfrac{M}{V}$

Problem: $\dfrac{102 \text{ g}}{6.20 \text{ cm}^3}$

Answer: _____

3. A king's crown has a volume of 111 cm³ and a mass of 1,999 g. Will it float in liquid water, which has a density of 1.00 g/cm³? Show your work below.

Formula: Density = $\dfrac{\text{Mass}}{\text{Volume}}$ or $D = \dfrac{M}{V}$

Problem: $\dfrac{1{,}999 \text{ g}}{111 \text{ cm}^3}$

Answer: _____

The density of gold is 19.3 g/cm³. Is the crown pure gold? Explain your answer.

_____

_____

4. A 6.0 cm³ sample of aluminum has a mass of 12.5 g. Will it float in liquid water, which has a density of 1.00 g/cm³? Show your work below.

Formula: Density = $\dfrac{\text{Mass}}{\text{Volume}}$ or $D = \dfrac{M}{V}$

Problem: $\dfrac{12.5 \text{ g}}{6.0 \text{ cm}^3}$

Answer: _____

Name: _____   Date: _____

ARCHIMEDES' PRINCIPLE
Apply

Matching

_____ 1. fluid

_____ 2. buoyancy

_____ 3. density

_____ 4. displacement

_____ 5. Archimedes' Principle

a. is the tendency of certain objects to float or rise in fluid

b. a body immersed in a fluid experiences a buoyant force equal to the weight of the fluid it displaces

c. any material, either liquid or gas, that can flow

d. is the relationship between the mass and volume of an object

e. a method used to find the volume of an irregular object

Work It Out

You are given a sample of a solid that has a mass of 10 g and a volume of 3.6 cm^3. Will it float in liquid water, which has a density of 1.00 g/cm^3? Show your work below.

Answer: _____

Critical Thinking

Why do icebergs float in the ocean?

_____

_____

_____

_____

_____

_____

Multiple Choice

Use the illustration at the right to answer the questions below.

1. Which statement is true about the volume of the water displaced when the egg was dropped into the glass?

   a. It is equal to the volume of the egg.
   b. It is greater than the volume of the egg.
   c. It is less than the volume of the egg.
   d. It is twice the volume of the egg.

2. What do you know about the buoyant force on the egg?

   a. It is equal to the density of the water displaced.
   b. It is equal to the volume of the water displaced.
   c. It is less than the weight of the water displaced.
   d. It is equal to the weight of the water displaced.

Name: _____ Date: _____

ARCHIMEDES' PRINCIPLE
Investigate

Activity #1—Sink or Float?
Materials: pennies, large pan, water, aluminum foil
Procedure:

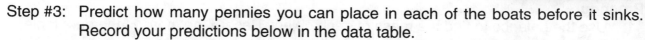

Step #1: Fill the pan with water.
Step #2: Construct three boats of different sizes from the aluminum foil.
Step #3: Predict how many pennies you can place in each of the boats before it sinks. Record your predictions below in the data table.
Step #4: Add pennies to each boat until it sinks. Record the number of pennies it took to sink each boat below.

Results:

Boat:	Boat #1	Boat #2	Boat #3
Number of Pennies Predicted:			
Actual Number of Pennies:			

Conclusion: Does the boat size influence the number of pennies it can carry? _____

_____

Activity #2—Toy Boat
Materials: toy boat that will float, coffee can, large pan, balance scale, water, small container
Procedure:

Step #1: Weigh the toy boat and the empty large pan. Record the measurements in the data table below.
Step #2: Punch a hole in the coffee can about one inch from its top rim. Fill the can until water flows from the hole.
Step #3: After the water has stopped flowing out, put the coffee can in the larger pan.
Step #4: Place the toy boat in the can.
Step #5: Weigh the large pan and the water that has overflowed from the coffee can, and record the measurement below.

Results:

Weight of Boat (g):	Weight of Large Pan Without Water (g)	Weight of Large Pan With Water (g)

Conclusion: _____

_____

Name: _____ Date: _____

ARCHIMEDES' PRINCIPLE
Inquiry Lab

Purpose: Determine if density affects an object's ability to float.

Materials:

plastic tub $\frac{1}{2}$ to $\frac{3}{4}$ full of water	15 mL water
various small objects (blocks, balls, rocks, etc)	balance scale
masses for scale	graduated cylinder

Procedure:

1. Use the balance to find the mass of each object. Record the mass in the data table.
2. Add 15 mL of water to the graduated cylinder.
3. Calculate the volume of each object. Record the volume in the data table.
4. Calculate the density of each object by dividing the mass by the volume.

Results: **Mass, Volume, Density**

Object	Mass (g)	Volume (mL)	Density M/V (g/mL)

5. Using the information in the data table above, predict and record below which objects will sink and which ones will float.
6. Record the density of each object in the data table below.
7. Test your predictions by placing each item in the tub of water, and record the actual results below.

Results: **Sink or Float**

Object	Predictions: Sink/Float	Actual: Sink/Float	Density

Conclusion: _____
_____
_____
_____

UNIT 3: SCIENTIFIC PRINCIPLES
Lesson 2: Pascal's Principle

My work is all about pressure.

Pascal's Principle

Pascal's Principle states that a change in the pressure applied to an enclosed container is transmitted without change throughout the fluid and acts in all directions.

Hydrodynamics

Pascal worked in the field of **hydrodynamics**, which deals with the power of moving fluids. His inventions include the hydraulic press (using hydraulic pressure to multiply force) and the syringe.

Blaise Pascal (1623–1662) was a French mathematician, physicist, and philosopher.

Hydraulic Lifts

Hydraulics is the science of applying Pascal's Principle. You might be surprised to know the force pushing a car upward by a hydraulic lift is being exerted by a fluid. The hydraulic lift uses the confined fluid to transfer pressure from one platform to another.

Pressure is applied on the fluid in the small cylinder.

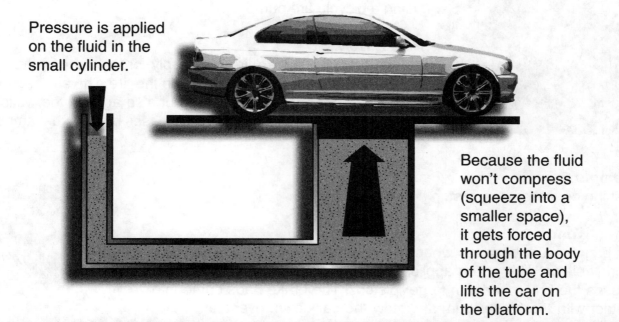

Because the fluid won't compress (squeeze into a smaller space), it gets forced through the body of the tube and lifts the car on the platform.

PASCAL'S PRINCIPLE
Knowledge Builder

Pressure and Fluids

Terms

- **fluid:** any substance that has no definite shape and has the ability to flow; liquid, gas, and plasma
- **pressure:** a force that is exerted uniformly in all directions
- **transmitted:** sent out

Hydrodynamics

Hydrodynamics deals with the power of moving fluids. Pushing on the fluid can increase pressure that is transmitted through the fluid.

Example 1:
Squeezing a tube of toothpaste

How It Works:
A force was applied when you squeezed the tube. This increased the pressure in the fluid and pushed the toothpaste out the opening.

Example 2:
Using a bicycle tire pump

How It Works:
When you pump a bike tire, you apply force on the pump that in turn exerts a force on the air inside the tire. The air responds by pushing not only on the pump but also against the walls of the tire. As a result, the pressure increases by an equal amount throughout the tire.

Example 3:
Pushing on the brakes to stop a car

How It Works:
Car brakes work because when you push the brake pedal, it pushes a small piston. The piston applies pressure on the brake fluid, which presses the brake pads on larger pistons. The brake pads come into contact with the brake drum and slow the car down, eventually stopping the car.

Name: _____ Date: _____

PASCAL'S PRINCIPLE
Apply

Matching

_____ 1. hydraulics

_____ 2. hydrodynamics

_____ 3. pressure

_____ 4. fluid

_____ 5. transmit

a. sent out

b. any substance that has no definite shape and has the ability to flow; liquid, gas, and plasma

c. deals with the power of moving fluids

d. a force that is exerted uniformly in all directions

e. the science of applying Pascal's Principle

Fill in the Blanks

1. Pascal's Principle states that a change in the _____ applied to an enclosed container is _____ without change throughout the _____ and acts in all directions.

2. The hydraulic lift uses the confined _____ to transfer pressure from one platform to another.

3. When you push the brake pedal of a car, it pushes a small piston filled with brake _____.

4. Squeezing a toothpaste tube increases the _____ in the fluid and pushes the toothpaste out the opening.

5. Applying force on a bicycle tire pump exerts a force on the _____ inside the tire.

Constructed Response

1. How would you describe a substance that can flow? _____

_____

2. How does a hydraulic system increase force? _____

_____

3. How are forces transmitted through fluids? _____

_____

Critical Thinking

Why do you think a liquid is used in a hydraulic lift? Answer on your own paper.

Name: _____ Date: _____

PASCAL'S PRINCIPLE
Investigate

Activity #1—Balloons and Pascal

Materials: balloon

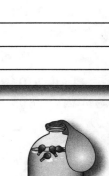

Procedure:

Step #1: Blow up a balloon and tie a knot in the end.

Step #2: Firmly press down on the balloon with your foot, but not hard enough to pop the balloon.

Observations:

What happened to the balloon? _____

_____

Conclusion:

How did this activity demonstrate Pascal's principle?

_____

_____

_____

Activity #2—Diving Matches (adult supervision needed with matches)

Materials: 5 wooden matches, 1-liter bottle, rubber balloon, water

Procedure:

Step #1: Prepare the matchsticks by cutting off the combustible heads and discarding the wooden sticks.

Step #2: Fill the bottle to the brim with water.

Step #3: Drop the matchstick heads into the bottle.

Step #4: Place the mouth of the balloon tightly over the bottle's opening.

Step #5: Press the balloon 'diaphragm' covering the mouth of the bottle between two fingers.

Observations:

What happens to the match heads? _____

_____

Conclusion:

How did this activity demonstrate Pascal's principle? _____

_____

_____

_____

UNIT 3: SCIENTIFIC PRINCIPLES
Lesson 3: Bernoulli's Principle

Bernoulli's Principle

Bernoulli's Principle states that in fluid flow, an increase in velocity causes a decrease in pressure. This means the faster a fluid flows, the less pressure it exerts.

The faster air flows, the less pressure it exerts.

Daniel Bernoulli (1700–1782) was a Dutch-Swiss mathematician. His most important work describes the relationship between fluid flow, pressure, and velocity.

Fluids

Physical scientists describe **fluids** as any substance that has no definite shape and has the ability to flow. Liquid, gas, and plasma are fluids. The molecules that make up these fluids do exert a pressure on surfaces with which they come in contact. Fluids move from an area of high pressure to one of low pressure.

Lift

Bernoulli's Principle helps explain that an aircraft can achieve **lift** (upward force) because of the shape of its wings. They are shaped so that air flows faster over the top of the wing and slower underneath. Fast-moving air equals low air pressure while slow-moving air equals high air pressure. The high air pressure underneath the wings will therefore push the aircraft up through the lower air pressure.

Lower pressure is caused by the increased speed of the air over the wing.

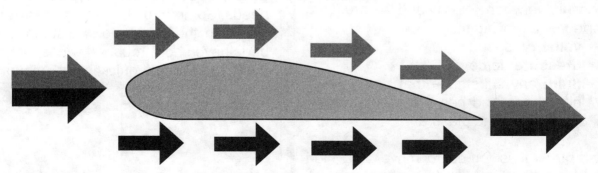

Since the pressure is higher beneath the wing, the wing is pushed upwards.

BERNOULLI'S PRINCIPLE
Knowledge Builder

Pressure and Fluids

Bernoulli's Principle—Air

Bernoulli's Principle can be used to explain the damage caused by violent storms.

Remember: The pressure in a fluid decreases as the speed of the fluid increases.

During violent storms, such as hurricanes or tornados, high-speed winds make air pressure outside drop. The air pressure in a house then becomes higher than outside the house. The pressure difference is enough to lift the roof or explode windows.

Terms

Bernoulli's Principle describes the relationship between velocity and the pressure exerted by a moving fluid.
- **velocity:** speed
- **pressure:** force
- **fluid:** any substance that has no definite shape and has the ability to flow: liquid, gas, and plasma

Example: Air is forced to move at a high speed from the tube of a hair dryer.

Bernoulli's Principle—Liquid

Bernoulli's Principle can be used to explain why water spurts faster from a hose if you put your thumb over the opening.

Remember: An increase in fluid velocity coincides with a decrease in pressure.

The reason the water spurts faster from a hose if you put your thumb over the opening is because the same volume of water per second must pass through the opening, and if the opening is smaller, the velocity must be higher.

Wings and Flight

Bernoulli's Principle helps explain why birds can fly. A bird's wings provide lift in the same way that an airplane wing does.

Not all birds have the same shaped wings. It depends on the type of flight a bird needs. Some birds have long, narrow wings that help them glide long distances. Some birds have short, rounded wings that enable them to take off quickly and make sharp turns.

Name: _____   Date: _____

BERNOULLI'S PRINCIPLE
Apply

Matching

_____ 1. Bernoulli's Principle   a. any substance that has no definite shape and has the ability to flow

_____ 2. fluid   b. force

_____ 3. velocity   c. upward force

_____ 4. pressure   d. speed

_____ 5. lift   e. states that in fluid flow, an increase in velocity causes a decrease in pressure

Fill in the Blanks

1. Bernoulli's Principle describes the relationship between _____ and the _____ exerted by a moving _____.

2. Fast-moving air equals _____ air pressure, while slow-moving air equals _____ air pressure.

3. The pressure in a fluid _____ as the speed of the fluid increases.

4. The _____ a fluid flows, the less pressure it exerts.

5. Bernoulli's Principle helps explain that an aircraft can achieve _____ because of the shape of its wings.

Multiple Choice

1. How do long, narrow wings help a bird?
   a. helps them to take off quickly (lift)
   b. helps them make sharp turns
   c. helps them find food
   d. helps them glide long distances

2. Why does water spurt faster from a hose when you put your thumb over the end?
   a. the opening is smaller, so the velocity must be higher
   b. the opening is larger, so the velocity must be higher
   c. the opening is smaller, so the velocity must be lower
   d. the opening is larger, so the velocity must be lower

Critical Thinking

Why do airplanes have different wing shapes?

_____

_____

_____

_____

_____

_____

_____

Name: _____   Date: _____

BERNOULLI'S PRINCIPLE
Investigate

Activity #1—Kissing Ping-Pong Balls

Materials:
>   2 ping-pong balls   2 pieces of string (20 cm each)   masking tape

Procedure:

Step #1: Tape each piece of string to the ping-pong balls.

Step #2: Hang the balls from a level horizontal bar, keeping the balls about 3 cm apart.

Step #3: Place your mouth between the two balls about 6 to 8 cm from them.

Step #4: Blow a steady stream of air between them.

Observations: _____

_____

_____

Conclusion:

How did this activity demonstrate Bernoulli's Principle? _____

_____

_____

_____

Activity #2—Air Pressure

Materials: hair dryer   ping-pong ball   empty toilet paper tube

Procedure:

Step #1: Turn the hair dryer on high and point it toward the ceiling. Use a cool-air setting.

Step #2: Place the ping-pong ball into the stream of air.

Step #3: Slowly lower an empty toilet paper tube over the ball.

Observations:

What happened to the ping-pong ball? _____

_____

_____

Conclusion:

How did this activity demonstrate Bernoulli's Principle? _____

_____

_____

_____

Answer Keys

Unit 1: Scientific Theories

Atomic Theory of Matter
Apply (p. 6)
Matching
1. d   2. c   3. f   4. e   5. a   6. b

Fill in the Blanks
1. Democritus   2. Electrons
3. solids, liquids, gases, plasma
4. Atomic, Theory   5. Protons, neutrons

Multiple Choice
1. d   2. b

Constructed Response
1. Electrons move in energy levels.
2. Dalton discovered the Atomic Theory on which all current understandings of the atom are based

Critical Thinking
Answers will vary but may include: Democritus thought that the atom was indivisible. He thought that everything in the universe was made up of only one thing that was so tiny and that he called atoms. The word *atom* came from the Greek word *atomos* meaning "indivisible."

Cell Theory
Apply (p. 10)
Matching
1. d   2. c   3. e   4. b   5. a

Fill in the Blanks
1. cell membrane, nucleus, cytoplasm
2. cells   3. Robert Hooke
4. units/blocks   5. living

Constructed Response
1. They are single cells with a nucleus.
2. Bacteria are organisms made up of only one cell.

Critical Thinking
Answers will vary but may include: Viruses are an exception to the Cell Theory. They are considered alive by some scientists, yet they are not made up of cells. Viruses have many features of life, but by definition of the Cell Theory, they are not alive. They are basically made up of proteins.

Investigate (p. 11)
The plant cell is in the box. The box represents the cell wall.

Unit 2: Scientific Laws

Periodic Law
Apply (p. 19)
Matching
1. e   2. c   3. a   4. b   5. d

Fill in the Blanks
1. Transition   2. alkaline earth metal
3. actinide   4. BCNO
5. halogen   6. noble gases
7. lanthanide   8. alkali metal

Uses of Elements
1. gallium, rhenium, mercury
2. beryllium, carbon, aluminum, silicon, chromium, copper, zirconium, ytterbium, platinum, gold, silver
3. fluorine
4. silicon, zinc, gallium, germanium, gadolinium, terbium, tantalum, tungsten

Element Symbols
1. Fe   2. Ag   3. K   4. Au
5. Na   6. He   7. H

Investigate (p. 20)
Activity #1—Elements
Oxygen
1. 8   2. 0   3. 16
4. BCNO   5. Gas
6. Nonmetal   7. Natural
8. Stable
Uranium
9. 92   10. U   11. 3
12. Actinide   13. Solid
14. Metal   15. Natural
16. Radioactive
Activity #2—Element Symbols
1. Mg   2. Pb   3. Cl   4. C
5. O   6. S   7. Si   8. Cu
9. I   10. Ni
11. Silver   12. Aluminum
13. Gold   14. Carbon

15. Calcium   16. Phosphorus
17. Mercury   18. Iron
19. Hydrogen   20. Helium

Activity #3–Families
1. transition element   2. noble gases
3. BCNO   4. alkali metal family
5. halogen   6. BCNO
7. alkaline earth family
8–12. Answers may vary. Possible answers
   include:
8. drinking cans   9. disinfectant in water
10. color T.V.   11. fuel for nuclear power
12. rocket nose cones

Newton's Laws of Motion
Understanding Formulas (p. 25)
1. 8 m/s/s   2. 18,000 N   3. 1,500 kg
4. 12 N

Apply (p. 26)
Matching
1. c   2. e   3. a   4. b   5. d
Multiple Choice
1. c   2. c
Work It Out
5 N
Constructed Response
The propeller pushing backward on the water is the
force. The water pushing forward on the propeller is
the reaction. The propeller exerts the force. The water reacts, and the boat is pushed forward.

Investigate (p. 27)
Activity #1–First Law of Motion
Results: As the ruler hits the bottom checker, the
   checker slides out of the way without knocking
   over the rest of the tower.
Conclusion: Answers will vary but may include: The
   remaining checkers are not acted upon by the
   force of the ruler, so they remain at rest.

Activity #2–Second Law of Motion
Conclusion: Answers will vary but may include: Mass
   affects the distance an object will travel.

Activity # 3–Third Law of Motion
Results: When the balloon is released, it moves forward.

Conclusion: Answers will vary but may include: The
   action is the air inside the balloon rushing out.
   The reaction is the balloon moving forward.

Inquiry Lab (p. 28)
Answers will vary but may include: The greater the
mass of an object, the greater the speed due to inertia.

Law of Conservation of Momentum
Understanding Formulas (p. 31)
1. 5 m/s   2. 640 kg·m/sec

Apply (p. 32)
Matching
1. d   2. e   3. a   4. c   5. b
Fill in the Blanks
1. stop   2. weigh   3. motion
4. transferred   5. momentum
Work It Out
378 kg·m/sec
Constructed Response
The taxi has more momentum because it weighs
more than the baseball.

Investigation (p. 33)
Activity #1–Marbles
Observations: The last marble in the line moves forward.
Conclusion: Answers will vary but may include: The
   energy from the rolled marble is transferred to
   the three other marbles.

Activity #2–Bouncing Balls
Conclusion: Answers will vary but may include: Momentum is related to mass and velocity. The large
   ball transfers its momentum, even when moving
   slowly, so the small ball travels faster.

Law of Universal Gravitation
Understanding Formulas (p.36)
1. 1,765.8 N/kg   2. 833.85 N/kg

Understanding Formulas (p. 37)
Determine the Distance an Object Falls
3. 9; 44.1   4. 16; 78.4   5. 25; 122.5

Understanding Formulas (p. 38)
Speed
1. 19.6   2. 49   3. 78.4

Apply (p. 39)
Matching
1. c   2. e   3. a   4. b   5. d
Multiple Choice
1. c   2. b
Work It Out
8,338.5 N/kg
Constructed Response
The pull of gravity on Jupiter is greater than the pull of gravity on Earth.

Balance the Coefficient (p. 42)
1. $8H + 2O_2 \longrightarrow 4H_2O$
2. $12Na + 6Cl_2 \longrightarrow 12NaCl$
3. $4C + 4O_2 \longrightarrow 4CO_2$
4. $3Fe + 3S \longrightarrow 3FeS$
5. $4Mg + 2O_2 \longrightarrow 4MgO$

Law of Conservation of Matter
Apply (p. 43)
Matching
1. f   2. d   3. a   4. b   5. c   6. e
Work it Out
$2H_2 + 2Br_2 \longrightarrow 4HBr$
Bonus: hydrogen bromide
Multiple Choice
1. b   2. b
Constructed Response
The mass of the wood and the oxygen that allowed it to burn will equal the mass of the ash and smoke (gases) given off during the burning.

Investigate (p. 44)
Activity #1–Change in Matter
Observation: gas released
Conclusion: Answers will vary but may include: Gas is an invisible product of the chemical reaction. Its mass is often forgotten when calculating the final mass.

Activity #2–Chemical Reaction
Observation: bag inflated
Conclusion: Answers will vary but may include: Mass cannot be created nor destroyed. A gas is formed, which will inflate the bag. The mass of the sealed bag must be determined in order to ascertain if there has been any change in the mass of the reactants and product before and after the reaction took place.

Laws of Thermodynamics
Apply (p. 47)
Matching
1. b   2. d   3. a   4. e   5. c
Fill in the Blanks
1. kinetic, potential   2. heat
3. Conservation   4. heat capacity
5. warm, cold
Constructed Response
The Second Law of Thermodynamics explains how heat moves. Since heat is energy, heat flows from warm objects to cold objects, thus spreading out.
Complete the Chart
1. radiation   2. conduction   3. convection
4. conduction   5. convection

Investigation (p. 48)
Activity #1–Rubber Band
Observation: The rubber band was warm.
Conclusion: Answers will vary but may include: By stretching the rubber band, a force was applied through a distance. Work was being done. Some of that work went into changing the potential energy of the band, while some went into heat. This added heat changed the temperature of the band.

Activity #2–Heat Transfer
Observation: The water stopped boiling.
Conclusion: Answers will vary but may include: According to the Second Law of Thermodynamics, the heat coming from the burner will always flow to the coldest object in the pan—in this case the ice cube.

Kepler's Three Laws of Planetary Motion
Apply (p.51)
Matching
1. e   2. d   3. b   4. c   5. a

Fill in the Blanks
1. Isaac Newton   2. *Somnium*
3. distance   4. focus
5. closer, slowly

Multiple Choice
1. c   2. b

Critical Thinking
Answers will vary but may include: Johannes Kepler was able to describe planetary motions more precisely with his three Laws.

Investigate (p. 52–54)
Activity #1 & #3
Teacher check labeling and measurements.

Activity #2–Eccentricity
1. 0.58   2. 0.81   3. 0.89

Mendel's Laws of Genetics
Apply (p. 57)
Matching
1. e   2. b   3. d   4. c   5. a

Fill in the Blanks
1. Heredity is where a gene from the father and a gene from the mother are passed onto their offspring.
2. Answers will vary but may include: Mendel discovered how genes work and that they directly impact what offspring will look like.

Work It Out

Dd	Dd
Dd	Dd

1. Dd   2. 100% or 4/4

Critical Thinking
Answers will vary but may include: Heredity is the passing of traits from parent to offspring. A child receives a combination of traits from both parents, making him or her a new and unique individual.

Unit 3: Scientific Principles

Archimedes' Principle
Understanding Formulas (p. 61)
1. 1.79 g/cm^3; The density of the sample is greater than the density of water. The sample will sink.
2. 16.45 g/cm^3; The density of the sample is greater than the density of water. The sample will sink.
3. 18.01 g/cm^3; The density of the sample is greater than the density of water. The sample will sink. The crown is not pure gold. Their densities are not the same.
4. 2.08 g/cm^3; The density of the sample is greater than the density of water. The sample will sink.

Apply (p. 62)
Matching
1. c   2. a   3. d   4. e   5. b

Work it Out
2.78 g/cm^3; The density is greater than the density of water. It will not float.

Multiple Choice
1. a   2. c

Critical Thinking
Answers will vary but may include: Weight is a force in the downward direction. The buoyant force is in the upward direction. An object will float if the upward force is equal to the weight of the object.

Investigate (p. 63)
Activity #1–Sink or Float?
Conclusion: Yes, the larger the boat, the more pennies it will hold.

Activity #2–Toy Boat
Conclusion: The weight of the boat is equal to the weight of the water it displaces.

Inquiry Lab (p.64)
Answers will vary but may include: Density is a physical property of matter that expresses a relationship of mass to volume. The more mass an object contains in a given space, the denser it is. If an object is less dense than the fluid in which it is placed, it will float. If it is more dense than the fluid, it will sink.

Pascal's Principle
Apply (p. 67)
Matching
1. e   2. c   3. d   4. b   5. a

Fill in the Blanks
1. pressure, transmitted, fluid
2. fluid   3. fluid
4. pressure   5. air

Constructed Response
1. a fluid
2. Pressure is applied to a fluid.
3. Pressure is sent out uniformly in all directions.

Critical Thinking
Answers will vary but may include: Pressure is applied on the fluid in a cylinder. Because the fluid won't compress, it gets forced through a pipe and lifts a heavy object on the platform.

Investigate (p. 68)
Activity #1–Ballons and Pascal
Observation: The balloon bulged out on all sides under the foot.
Conclusion: Answers will vary but may include: The air (fluid) was confined by the balloon. Pressure was applied by the foot. The pressure was sent out uniformly in all directions, causing the balloon to bulge out on all sides.

Activity #2–Diving Matches
Observation: The matches floated on top of the water, but when the diaphragm was pressed, they sank slowly to the bottom. When the pressure is lifted, the matches floated up again.
Conclusion: Answers will vary but may include: Pressure is transmitted through the water, forcing the matches to sink, and when the pressure is removed, the matches rise.

Bernoulli's Principle
Apply (p. 71)
Matching
1. e   2. a   3. d   4. b   5. c

Fill in the Blanks
1. velocity, pressure, fluid   2. low, high
3. decreases   4. faster
5. lift

Multiple Choice
1. d   2. a

Critical Thinking
Answers may vary but may include: An aircraft can achieve lift because of the shape of its wings. They are shaped so that air flows faster over the tops of the wings and slower underneath. Fast-moving air equals low air pressure, while slow-moving air equals high air pressure. The high air pressure underneath the wings will therefore push the aircraft up through the lower air pressure. Depending on what the purpose of the plane is, the shape of the wing will change to lift the weight of the plane.

Investigate (p. 72)
Activity #1–Kissing Ping-Pong Balls
Observation: The two ping-pong balls bump together.
Conclusion: Answers will vary but may include: The air moving between the two ping-pong balls reduces the air pressure.

Activity #2–Air Pressure
Observation: The ball stayed in the air stream of the hair dryer. When the empty toilet paper tube was placed into the air stream, the ball was sucked up into the tube.
Conclusion: Answers will vary but may include: When you place the ball in the stream of air created by the hair dryer, you force the air to flow around the ball and created an area of lower pressure. The still air surrounding the air stream has more pressure and pushes the ball to keep it in the stream. When you place the empty toilet paper tube into the air stream, the air is funneled into a smaller area, making air move even faster. The pressure in the tube becomes even lower than that of the air surrounding the ball, and the ball is sucked up into the tube.

Bibliography

Books

Abbgy, Theodore S. *Elements and the Periodic Table.* Quincy, IL: Mark Twain Media/Carson-Dellosa Publishing LLC. 2001.

Atkins, Peter. *The Laws of Thermodynamics: A Very Short Introduction.* New York: Oxford University Press, USA. 2010.

Boerst, William J. *Johannes Kepler: Discovering the Laws of Celestial Motion.* Greensboro, NC: Morgan Reynolds Pub. 2003.

Darrigol, Olivier. *Worlds of Flow: A History of Hydrodynamics from the Bernoullis to Prandtl.* Oxford, UK: Oxford University Press. 2005.

Daubeny, Charles. *An Introduction to the Atomic Theory.* Nabu Press. 2010. (Reproduction of 1850 edition published by Oxford University Press)

Girifalco, Louis. *The Universal Force: Gravity—Creator of Worlds.* Oxford, UK: Oxford University Press. 2007.

Gordin, Michael D. *A Well-Ordered Thing: Dmitri Mendeleev and the Shadow of the Periodic Table.* New York: Basic Books. 2004.

Hollihan, Kerrie Logan. *Isaac Newton and Physics for Kids: His Life and Ideas with 21 Activities.* Chicago: Chicago Review Press, Inc. 2009.

Introduction to Physical Science. New York: Glencoe/McGraw-Hill. 2005.

Krebs, Robert, E. *Encyclopedia of Scientific Principles, Laws, and Theories.* Santa Barbara, CA: Greenwood Press. 2008.

Klare, Roger. *Gregor Mendel: Father of Genetics.* Berkeley Heights, NJ: Enslow Publishers. 1997.

Raham, Gary. *Science Tutor: Earth & Space Science.* Quincy, IL: Mark Twain Media/Carson-Dellosa Publishing LLC. 2006.

Raham, Gary. *Science Tutor: Physical Science.* Quincy, IL: Mark Twain Media/Carson-Dellosa Publishing LLC. 2006.

Shireman, Myrl. *Physical Science.* Quincy, IL: Mark Twain Media/Carson-Dellosa Publishing LLC. 1997.

Websites

"Cool Science." Howard Hughes Medical Institute. < http://www.hhmi.org/coolscience/>.

"How Stuff Works." Discovery Communications, LLC. <http://www.howstuffworks.com/>.

"Science News for Kids." Society for Science & the Public. <http://www.sciencenewsforkids.org/>.

"Zoomsci." Public Broadcasting Service. < http://pbskids.org/zoom/activities/sci/>.